Educational Design Research

Educational design research is the systematic study of designing, developing, and evaluating educational programs, processes, and products. It can be an invaluable process, yielding considerable insight into how to optimize educational interventions and better understand teaching and learning. However, the fact that such investigations are typically carried out in naturalistic settings – with all the color and complexity that accompany real classrooms and schools – presents researchers with significant methodological challenges, and scientific rigor can be difficult to maintain. This book addresses a clear and growing need to better understand and address the challenges faced by educational design researchers.

Educational Design Research has been written to appeal to the rapidly growing international audience of educational researchers who situate their studies in practice. The publication contains four main parts, plus supplementary materials available on a companion website. First, a mixture of substantive information is presented for those interested in learning about the essence of design research. The second part of the book features examples of design research, and in the third, researchers share their views on quality assurance. Finally, policy implications are offered and discussed, with particular attention paid to understanding and evaluating design research work.

Altogether, this book provides an informative and instructive platform for considering the domain of design research in education. Anyone with an interest in educational research will find it essential reading.

Jan van den Akker is Professor at the Department of Curriculum, University of Twente, the Netherlands, and Director of the National Institute for Curriculum Development.

Koeno Gravemeijer is Professor at the Faculty of Social Sciences, University of Utrecht, the Netherlands.

Susan McKenney is Assistant Professor at the Department of Curriculum, University of Twente, the Netherlands.

Nienke Nieveen is Assistant Professor at the Department of Curriculum, University of Twente, the Netherlands.

Educational Design Research

Edited by Jan van den Akker,
Koeno Gravemeijer,
Susan McKenney and
Nienke Nieveen

Routledge
Taylor & Francis Group

LONDON AND NEW YORK

First published 2006 by Routledge
2 Park Square, Milton Park, Abingdon, Oxon OX14 4RN.

Simultaneously published in the USA and Canada by Routledge
270 Madison Ave., New York, NY10016

Routledge is an imprint of the Taylor & Francis Group, an informa business

© 2006 Jan van den Akker, Koeno Gravemeijer, Susan McKenney and
Nienke Nieveen selection and editorial matter; individual chapters, the
contributors.

Typeset in Sabon and Gill Sans by Bookcraft Ltd, Stroud, Gloucestershire
Printed and bound in Great Britain by The Cromwell Press, Trowbridge, Wiltshire

British Library Cataloguing in Publication Data
A catalogue record for this book is available from the British Library

Library of Congress Cataloging in Publication Data
Educational design research / edited by Jan van den Akker [et al.].
    p. cm.
  Includes bibliographical references and index.
  1. Instructional systems—Design—Research. I. Akker, J. J. H. van den, 1950–
LB 1028.38.E38 2006
371.1007—dc22
2006007945

ISBN10: 0–415–39634–4 (hbk)
ISBN10: 0–415–39635–2 (pbk)
ISBN10: 0–203–08836–0 (ebk)
ISBN13: 978–0–415–39634–9 (hbk)
ISBN13: 978–0–415–39635–6 (pbk)
ISBN13: 978–0–203–08836–4 (ebk)

Contents

Illustrations

Tables

Contributors

Jan van den Akker (also editor) is Professor and Head of the Department of Curriculum (Faculty of Behavioral Sciences) at the University of Twente. Since the summer of 2005 he has been serving as Executive Director at the Netherlands Institute for Curriculum Development (SLO). In his wide teaching, research, supervision, and consultancy experiences (both in the Netherlands and abroad) he tends to approach curriculum design challenges from a broader educational innovation perspective. Over the years his preference for design research has grown because of its strong combination of practical relevance and scholarly progress.

Hugh Burkhardt has led a series of international projects from Michigan State and Nottingham Universities, where the Shell Centre team takes an "engineering research" approach at the systemic end of design research. Here, imaginative design and systematic development, with theory as a guide and empirical evidence the ultimate arbiter, tools that make the system work better are produced. Many such "tools for change" (assessment instruments, teaching materials, etc.) are needed to turn goals of policy into outcomes in practice. Burkhardt's other interests include making school mathematics more functional for everyone. He remains occasionally active in particle physics.

Paul Cobb is Professor in the Department of Teaching and Learning at Vanderbilt University where he teaches courses in elementary mathematics methods, design research methodology, and the institutional setting of mathematics teaching. His research interests focus on instructional design, students' statistical reasoning, the classroom microculture, and the broader institutional setting of mathematics teaching. He has conducted a series of classroom design experiments in collaboration with Koeno Gravemeijer and has used the methodology more recently to investigate the process of supporting a group of mathematics teachers' learning as it is situated in the institutional settings in which they work.

Daniel Edelson is Associate Professor of Learning Sciences and Computer

Science at Northwestern University in the USA. He leads the Geographic Data in Education (GEODE) Initiative at Northwestern, which is dedicated to the improvement of earth and environmental science education through the integration of authentic inquiry into the science curriculum. Throughout his career, he has employed design research toward the improvement of curriculum and software design, professional development, and classroom implementation. His research interests include interest motivation, the application of research on learning in instructional design, and software interaction design for students and teachers.

Koeno Gravemeijer (also editor) is Research Coordinator at the Freudenthal Institute (Department of Mathematics of the Faculty of Science) and holds a private chair at the Department of Educational Sciences (Faculty of Social and Behavioral Sciences) at Utrecht University. His research interests concern the domain-specific instruction theory for realistic mathematics education (RME); design research as a research method; and the role of symbols, (computer) tools, and models in mathematics education. The point of departure, which runs as a continuous thread through his work, is that educational research and the actual improvement of mathematics education in schools are reflexively related.

Anthony E. Kelly is Professor and Head of the Instructional Technology Program at George Mason University in Virginia, USA. His research interests extend to research methodology design, and research at the intersection of cognitive neuroscience and education. He has a National Science Foundation grant on design research methods with Richard Lesh. A volume edited by both principal investigators on the topic of design research is forthcoming. Kelly edited the special issue on design research, *Educational Researcher*, vol. 32, 2003. He served as a program manager at the National Science Foundation from 1997–2000.

Susan McKenney (also editor) is Assistant Professor in the Department of Curriculum (Faculty of Behavioral Sciences) at the University of Twente in the Netherlands. McKenney's current research and teaching focus on curriculum development, teacher professional development and, often, the supportive role of computers in those processes. Careful design, evaluation, and revision of educational improvement initiatives is a recurring theme in her consultancy and research endeavors, most of which are situated in the Netherlands, India, or southern Africa.

Nienke Nieveen (also editor) is Assistant Professor in the Department of Curriculum (Faculty of Behavioral Sciences) at the University of Twente in the Netherlands. Her current research explores successful scenarios for school-wide and school-based curriculum improvement that incorporate productive relations between curriculum, teacher and school development. She actively incorporates the design research approach in research projects and in courses on educational design and evaluation.

D. C. Phillips is Professor of Education, and by courtesy Professor of Philosophy, at Stanford University. He is a member of the US National Academy of Education and a Fellow of the International Academy of Education. A philosopher of education and social science with a particular interest in research methodology, and history of nineteenth- and twentieth-century social science and educational theory, he is author, co-author, or editor of eleven books and numerous journal articles. His most recent book is *Postpositivism and Educational Research* (with N. Burbules).

Thomas Reeves teaches, conducts research, and provides service related to program evaluation, multimedia design, educational research, and other professional activities in the Department of Educational Psychology and Instructional Technology of the College of Education at the University of Georgia. For more than 20 years, he has been a vocal critic of traditional approaches to educational technology research as well as a proponent of alternative, more socially-responsive, approaches, including design research. He believes that educational researchers, especially those who work in publicly funded institutions, should pursue research goals that have a morally-defensive rationale for improving human well-being.

Decker Walker is Professor in the School of Education at Stanford University. His scholarly interests are in the study of curriculum and finding ways to improve the pre-college curriculum through the use of information technology (computers, video, telecommunications). He has published widely on curriculum development and evaluation, including *Fundamentals of Curriculum* (2000) and *Curriculum and Aims* (2004). His recent work concentrates on the role and meaning of information technology in education. He was a founding faculty member of the Learning Design and Technology program at Stanford and has served as Director of the program since 1997. His long-term interest in design research has heightened in recent years as design research has assumed a central role in the work of students and faculty in that program.

Acknowledgements

The roots for this book stem from an educational design research seminar organized by the Netherlands Organization for Scientific Research, in particular, its Program Council for Educational Research (NWO/PROO). This book was conceptualized during that seminar and contains chapters based on presentations and discussions from those fruitful days in Amsterdam. We therefore express our gratitude to Paul Berendsen, Hubert Coonen, Joris Voskuilen, and the staff at NWO/PROO for their interest and support in educational design research, and for bringing this group of scholars together.

Jan van den Akker
Koeno Gravemeijer
Susan McKenney
Nienke Nieveen

Part 1

What and why

Chapter 1

Introducing educational design research

Jan van den Akker, Koeno Gravemeijer,
Susan McKenney and Nienke Nieveen

Origins of this book

Design research has been gaining momentum in recent years, particularly in the field of educational studies. This has been evidenced by prominent journal articles (Burkhardt and Schoenfeld 2003), book chapters (Richey *et al.* 2004), as well as books (van den Akker *et al.* 1999) and special issues of journals dedicated specifically to the topic (*Educational Researcher* 32(1), 2003; *Journal of the Learning Sciences* 13(1), 2004), or to the more general need to revisit research approaches, including design research (*Journal of Computing in Higher Education* 16(2), 2005).

Definition of the approach is now beginning to solidify, but also to differentiate. As methodological guidelines and promising examples begin to surface with abundance, pruning becomes necessary (Kelly 2004). Dede (2004) as well as Gorard *et al.* (2004) call for the educational research community to seriously reflect on setting standards that improve the quality of this approach.

This book offers such a reflection. Most of its chapters are revised, updated, and elaborated versions of presentations given at a seminar held in Amsterdam, organized by the Dutch Program Council for Educational Research from the Netherlands Organization for Scientific Research (NWO/PROO). As a funding agency, NWO/PROO is interested in the clarification of what design research entails as well as articulation of quality standards and criteria to judge proposals and evaluate the outcomes of such research. The presentations and discussions during the seminar were very fruitful and stimulating. They provided the impetus to produce this book, which makes the findings available to a wider audience.

Motives for design research

The first and most compelling argument for initiating design research stems from the desire to *increase the relevance* of research for educational policy and practice. Educational research has long been criticized for its weak link with practice. Those who view educational research as a vehicle to inform improvement tend to take such criticism more seriously than those who argue that studies in the field of education should strive for knowledge in and of itself. Design research can contribute to more practical relevance. By carefully studying progressive approximations of ideal interventions in their target settings, researchers and practitioners construct increasingly workable and effective interventions, with improved articulation of principles that underpin their impact (Collins *et al.* 2004; van den Akker 1999). If successful in generating findings that are more widely perceived to be relevant and usable, the chances for improving policy are also increased.

A second motive for design research relates to scientific ambitions. Alongside directly practical applications and policy implications, design research aims at *developing empirically grounded theories* through combined study of both the process of learning and the means that support that process (diSessa and Cobb 2004; Gravemeijer 1994, 1998). Much of the current debate on design research concerns the question of how to justify such theories on the basis of design experiments. As the thrust to better understand learning and instruction in context grows, research must move from simulated or highly favorable settings toward more naturally occurring test beds (Barab and Squire 2004; Brown 1992).

A third motive relates to the aspiration of *increasing the robustness of design practice*. Many educational designers energetically approach the construction of innovative solutions to emerging educational problems, yet their understanding oftentimes remains implicit in the decisions made and the resulting design. From this perspective, there is a need to extract more explicit learning that can advance subsequent design efforts (Richey and Nelson 1996; Richey *et al.* 2004; Visscher-Voerman and Gustafson 2004).

About design research

In this book, we use *Design research* as a common label for a *family* of related research approaches with internal variations in aims and characteristics. It should be noted, however, that there are also many other labels to be found in literature, including (but not limited to) the following:

- *Design* studies, *Design* experiments
- *Development/Developmental* research
- *Formative* research, *Formative* evaluation
- *Engineering* research.

Clearly, we are dealing with an emerging trend, characterized by a proliferation of terminology and a lack of consensus on definitions (see van den Akker (1999) for a more elaborate overview). While the terminology has yet to become established, it is possible to outline a number of characteristics that apply to most design studies. Building on previous works (Cobb *et al.* 2003; Kelly 2003; Design-Based Research Collective 2003; Reeves *et al.* 2005; van den Akker 1999) design research may be characterized as:

- Interventionist: the research aims at designing an intervention in the real world;
- Iterative: the research incorporates a cyclic approach of design, evaluation, and revision;
- Process oriented: a black box model of input–output measurement is avoided, the focus is on understanding and improving interventions;
- Utility oriented: the merit of a design is measured, in part, by its practicality for users in real contexts; and
- Theory oriented: the design is (at least partly) based upon theoretical propositions, and field testing of the design contributes to theory building.

The following broad definition of Barab and Squire (2004) seems to be a generic one that encompasses most variations of educational design research: *"a series of approaches, with the intent of producing new theories, artifacts, and practices that account for and potentially impact learning and teaching in naturalistic settings."*

Further clarification of the nature of design research may be helped by a specification of what it is *not*. The most noteworthy aspect is probably that design researchers do *not* emphasize isolated variables. While design researchers do focus on specific objects and processes in specific contexts, they try to study those as integral and meaningful phenomena. The context-bound nature of much design research also explains why it usually does not strive toward context-free generalizations.

Inside this book

This book was created to appeal to the rapidly growing international audience of educational researchers who situate their studies in practice. The publication contains four main parts, plus supplemental materials available on the publisher's website. First, a mixture of substantive information is presented for those interested in learning about the essence of design research. This includes: its origins, applications for this approach, and discussion of benefits and risks associated with studies of this nature. The second part of the book features domain-specific perspectives on design research. Here, examples are given in terms of how this approach can serve the design of learning environments, educational technology, and curriculum. The third part of the book speaks to the issue of quality assurance. Three researchers express their thoughts on how to guard academic rigor while conducting design studies. In the last part of the book, policy implications are offered in broad terms, and specifically in terms of under-standing and evaluating design research work. While the book's supple-mental website contains additional information, its primary goal is to provide in-depth examples of high-quality design research. Together, the four book components and website provide an informative and instructive platform for considering the domain of design research in education.

References

Barab, S. and Squire, K. (2004). Design-based research: Putting a stake in the ground. *Journal of the Learning Sciences*, *13*(1), 1–14.

Brown, A. L. (1992). Design experiments: Theoretical and methodological challenges in creating complex interventions in classroom settings. *Journal of the Learning Sciences*, *2*(22), 141–78.

Burkhardt, H. and Schoenfeld, A. (2003). Improving educational research: Toward a more useful, more influential and better-funded enterprise. *Educational Researcher*, *32*(9), 3–14.

Cobb, P., Confrey, J., diSessa, A., Lehrer, R., and Schauble, L. (2003). Design experiments in educational research. *Educational Researcher*, *32*(1), 9–13.

Collins, A., Joseph, D., and Bielaczyc, K. (2004). Design research: Theoretical and methodological issues. *Journal of the Learning Sciences*, *13*(1), 15–42.

Dede, C. (2004). If design-based research is the answer, what is the question? *Journal of the Learning Sciences*, *13*(1), 105–14.

Design-Based Research Collective (2003). Design-based research: An emerging paradigm for educational inquiry. *Educational Researcher*, *32*(1), 5–8.

diSessa, A. A. and Cobb, P. (2004). Ontological innovation and the role of theory in design experiments. *Journal of the Learning Sciences*, *13*(1), 77–103.

Gorard, S., Roberts, K., and Taylor, C. (2004). What kind of creature is a design experiment? *British Educational Research Journal*, *30*(4), 577–90.

Gravemeijer, K. (1994) *Developing Realistic Mathematics Education*. Utrecht: Cdß Press.

Gravemeijer, K. (1998). Developmental research as a research method. In J. Kilpatrick and A. Sierpinska (eds), *Mathematics Education as a Research Domain: A Search for Identity* (pp. 277–95). Dordrecht: Kluwer Academic Publishers.

Kelly, A. (2003). Research as design. *Educational Researcher*, *32*(1), 3–4.

Kelly, A. (2004). Design research in education: Yes, but is it methodological? *Journal of the Learning Sciences*, *13*(1), 115–28.

Reeves, T., Herrington, J., and Oliver, R. (2005). Design research: A socially responsible approach to instructional technology research in higher education. *Journal of Computing in Higher Education*, *16*(2), 97–116.

Richey, R. and Nelson, W. (1996). Developmental research. In D. Jonassen (ed.), *Handbook of Research for Educational Communications and Technology* (pp. 1213–45). London: Macmillan.

Richey, R., Klein, J., and Nelson, W. (2004). Developmental research: Studies of instructional design and development. In D. Jonassen (ed.), *Handbook of Research for Educational Communications and Technology* (second edition) (pp. 1099–130). Bloomington, IN: Association for Educational Communications & Technology.

van den Akker, J. (1999). Principles and methods of development research. In J. van den Akker, R. Branch, K. Gustafson, N. Nieveen, and T. Plomp (eds), *Design Approaches and Tools in Education and Training* (pp. 1–14). Dordrecht: Kluwer Academic Publishers.

van den Akker, J., Branch, R., Gustafson, K., Nieveen, N., and Plomp, T. (eds) (1999). *Design Approaches and Tools in Education and Training*. Dordrecht: Kluwer Academic Publishers.

Visscher-Voerman, I. and Gustafson, K. (2004). Paradigms in the theory and practice of education and training design. *Educational Technology Research and Development*, 52(2), 69–89.

Chapter 2

Toward productive design studies

Decker Walker

Why now?

My thinking about design research begins with the question: Why now? Why have some researchers and policymakers become interested in design research at just this moment in history? I think that there are two major reasons. The most important is disappointment with the impact of conventional approaches to research in education. We have seen no intellectual breakthroughs in research in education comparable to advances in medicine, engineering, and the sciences; nor have we seen any measurable improvement in teaching practices or student learning on a large scale. In clinical experiments, practices and programs supposedly *backed by research* have generally proved to be only slightly better than conventional practice. In short, more than half a century of research into education since World War II has not noticeably improved education. In many countries the quality of education seems to have declined over the past several decades, just when educational research had supposedly begun to accumulate enough knowledge for its findings to make an impact. Many of us who advocate design research believe that it has the potential, in conjunction with standard forms of inquiry, to produce the kind of impact research has made in other areas of life, an argument I will develop later.

The second reason why some researchers and policymakers have begun to find design research attractive is the availability of promising new theories of learning and technologies through which these theories can be applied. Cognitive science, activity theory (or social constructionism), and brain research offer new perspectives on learning that may well be more powerful than the theories that have guided traditional research such as behaviorism, depth psychology (Freud, Jung, Adler, etc.), and conventional social psychology.

Some of these new theories make predictions about intricate details of learning that are not accessible to teachers and students in ordinary classroom situations. Others consider a much wider range of social influences and interactions than that which occurs in classrooms. New forms of educational intervention may be needed to realize practical benefits from these new theories. Fortunately, information and communication technologies have developed to the point where new technologically supported interactions may now be designed to apply and test these theories. Design research seems valuable, if not essential, in developing these new interventions.

How research influences practice

For most of its history, research in education has influenced practice only loosely and indirectly. Researchers taught theories and findings to educators – teachers, professional leaders, and researchers-in-training – and they in turn applied the theories. However, in practice theory and research findings often functioned as little more than slogans for reformers. Child-centered learning, discovery learning, and the project method, for instance, were, according to their advocates, said to be "based on research," but the range of practices included under their banners was so broad that each became more of a philosophy than a well-defined design. Occasionally theorists and researchers themselves actually designed concrete materials for teachers and students to use. Maria Montessori's preschool tasks, the look–say method of reading instruction, the initial teaching alphabet, standardized tests, and programmed instruction are well-known examples of materials designed by theorists and researchers. However, studies comparing research-based teaching methods or materials with conventional ones showed small effects or no statistically significant differences.

Design research envisions a tighter, more rigorous connection between learning principles and features of the educational innovation. In design research, a theorist or researcher's rigorous analysis of a learning problem leads to quite specific ideas for interventions. Designers then build systems that use information technology to create specific teaching and learning materials and methods designed to realize learning gains predicted by theory and research. If the theoretical analysis is right, then these interventions ought to give markedly more effective results. Designing these systems is an R&D endeavor, not a work of imagination or a straightforward deduction from theory. In order to create interventions, designers need to study how students and teachers actually respond to specific features of the design suggested by the theory. In other words, to show that a design rigorously implements principles from research and theory, designers must do design research.

Having shown that their design functions the way that theory predicts it should, designers need to try their design and see if its results really do live up to predictions. The first tests of any new design will most likely show weak results or none at all because designs need to be tuned and optimized to give best results. To be effective, any complex system normally requires a precise configuration of its elements. For instance, early radios worked – they would transmit and receive radio frequency signals – but they were weak and unreliable. Through design research, engineers discovered more effective ways to amplify the signal, sharpen the tuning, reduce noise, and make the radio's operation more reliable. It is only logical to suppose that the kind of research engineers do to improve the design of radios and other devices will also be needed to improve educational designs. (Of course, the kind of research needed for educational designs will be different from that conducted in engineering. Teachers and students are central to the functioning of educational practices and so design research in education needs methods drawn from the human sciences, arts, and humanities.)

In order to study the effectiveness of preliminary designs, design researchers need sound, reliable indicators of learning. Traditional tests created by teachers and conventional standardized tests are too crude and imprecise to test for the kinds of learning that the new theories envision. Design researchers have already developed a range of techniques for generating good indicators of learning, including close ethnographic observation, standard learning tasks with scoring rubrics, and other techniques for learning assessment. Assessment techniques are domain specific, that is, specific to the content and goals being taught, and so new techniques must be developed for each domain of learning and teaching. Developing or adapting assessments is an important part of the design research process. Figure 2.1 shows these relationships in a diagram.

Guidelines for good design studies

I believe that good design research will lead to more and better learning, hence the phrase *productive design studies* in the chapter title. Which research methods and approaches are most likely to lead to productive design research? For the most part, these methods will be drawn from established disciplines in the human sciences, arts, and humanities. I will mention several criteria that I would use to choose the methods that are most appropriate for design research studies.

Research ←→ Theory
    [**Design Research** with tighter, more rigorous connections]
        (leads to)   **Interventions (technology-based)**
            [**Design Research** on first generation interventions]
                (leads to)   **Improved practices & policies**
                    [**Design Research** on stronger, better indicators]
                        (leads to)   **More, better Learning**

Figure 2.1 How research improves practice

Riskier designs

Standards of methodological rigor traditionally applied to social science research are not, in my opinion, likely to lead to productive design research. Traditional standards are designed to test theories and for this purpose it is crucial to minimize the risk of accepting a false conclusion. Any mistake in research may lead to mistaken conclusions that hinder the growth of knowledge in the discipline. Any wrong turn in theory building can waste years of effort of the best scholars and researchers. In testing theories it pays to go to great lengths to get results that can withstand every criticism.

Design research is not done to test theories, even though its results can sometimes suggest weaknesses in theory. Rather, design research discovers ways to build systems based on theories and determine the effectiveness of these systems in practice. Design research therefore needs to balance boldness and caution in a different way. A super-cautious insistence on design studies that guard against every potential source of error will yield large, lengthy, expensive studies that delay designs and multiply their cost many times over. A series of smaller, less well-controlled studies may give results nearly as reliable, much faster and cheaper. Designers must deal simultaneously with many ambiguities and unknowns. It is often better for them to get a very preliminary result on several of these than to study one or two thoroughly while necessarily relying on guesswork, speculation, and assumptions for all the others. Design research that takes greater risks of accepting erroneous conclusions may have higher payoff. Less precise studies that do not fully disprove alternative hypotheses but look instead for a wide range of possible effects of complex designs may be sufficient to reveal ways to improve designs. This does not mean that anything goes. An overly bold approach that is full of unsubstantiated speculation provides little more than a random chance of hitting on the right design.

The key to productive design research is to strike a new balance between caution and risk-taking. Concentrate on the most important design problems, understand them thoroughly, identify the most promising features for the design in light of that understanding, build prototypes with these features, and try them out. This is a much bolder and riskier research strategy than conventional social science research methodologists recommend, but it stands a much better chance of leading to innovative designs.

Study cycles

Traditional approaches to research methods focus on individual studies. The goal is to design the best possible study to answer a given question. But design projects always face many questions and varying degrees of uncertainty about them. No single study can help with all, so the temptation is to focus on one question and do one study to answer that question. This leaves all the other questions completely open. A more sensible approach would be to identify the most important questions surrounding a particular design problem and plan a series of studies addressing each question. Begin each case with brief, inexpensive studies that give a general idea of the most promising approaches to the question. Then invest in studies (perhaps somewhat more intensive, expensive, and lengthy) of the questions that now seem most crucial. Confine the most rigorous (and therefore most expensive) studies to the last stage and the most crucial remaining questions.

Study resource requirements

All designs cost money, take time to implement, and require expertise and effort. A design may be successful in improving learning but at a prohibitive cost or only if taught by someone with a Ph.D. Resource requirements can and should be estimated and, in the case of programs already in operation, studied empirically. An aspect of every design study ought to be a consideration of the resources required to sustain the design.

Compare practices

The researcher's temptation is to study in great depth the *best* design, that is, the design option favored by the designer. However, designs advance best when the most promising options are compared to one another. Understanding one option deeply will still not tell the designer whether another option might be even better. So it is usually a good practice to compare the promise of all the reasonable design options and narrow the field to two or three of the most promising options, and then compare these directly in a study. Often the gold standard in education – the best way known to teach something – will be something like a human tutor – too expensive to provide for everyone. Still, it can be helpful to see how closely the new design approaches the gold standard. It is also often useful to compare the new design to conventional or accepted practice. The new design may not immediately offer better results than accepted practice, but it may cost a great deal less or it may be more easily improved or both.

Consider sustainability and robustness

A design that works in the laboratory may not work in the classroom. One that works in an experimental classroom may not work in a typical classroom. One that works when everything goes right may degrade drastically when teachers or students miss classes because of illness or when a teacher resigns and a new, untrained teacher is appointed, or under any of the countless circumstances that frequently occur in real life. Every form of practice degrades under severe conditions. We need designs that degrade gracefully rather than catastrophically. We need robust designs – ones that produce impressive results, not only under ideal conditions, but also under severe but realistic constraints. And we want sustainable designs that thrive and improve with time, not ones that slide downhill every year. Design research can estimate robustness and sustainability and can study them empirically once designs have been put in practice.

Involve stakeholders in judging design quality

Teachers may be more interested than others in how much work and effort will be required of them by a new program. Parents may be more interested than teachers in conflicts between what students learn in the new design and traditional religious or cultural beliefs. Civic leaders may be more interested in community involvement. Employers may be more interested in preparation for work. All these are legitimate concerns and the only way to ensure that everyone's concerns are considered in building a new design or studying it is to involve them in the process. This becomes especially important in judging the overall desirability of a design compared to accepted practices. The weighing of incommensurables involved in such a conclusion rules out an expert judgment and calls for the representation of the various viewpoints of those with the most stake in the matter.

Today's opportunity

Researchers today have an opportunity to pioneer design research and establish it as an essential part of the creation of new designs for learning and teaching. The alternative is a future in which designs are dominated by fashion and marketing considerations. I know of one prominent company, which produces learning software for children to be used in the home, whose design process consists of doing market research that leads to a design of the package the customer will see on the shelf. Several competing package designs are shown to focus groups of parents and eventually a design for the box is finalized. At this point, software developers are given the box and told to produce software to fit it. This might not be a bad way to start a design process if only the software developers were empowered to conduct further studies with children to develop software that actually fostered learning more effectively. Unfortunately, in this case and in so many others, the rest of the design process was done by the seat of the pants. If we researchers and academics want more carefully considered designs with established effectiveness, we have to show the way. Productive design research is the way.

Part 2

Examples from the field

Chapter 3

Design research from a learning design perspective

Koeno Gravemeijer and Paul Cobb

In this contribution, we want to elaborate on an approach to design research that has been used and refined in a series of design research projects in which the present authors collaborated over a 10-year period. To locate our contribution in this book, we may categorize our approach as falling within the broader category of design research that aims at creating innovative learning ecologies in order to develop local instruction theories on the one hand, and to study the forms of learning that those learning ecologies are intended to support on the other hand.[1] The research projects we focus on involve a research team taking responsibility for a group of students' learning for a period of time. All projects concern the domain of mathematics education (including statistics education).

The approach to design research, which we developed over the years, has its roots in the history of the two authors. One has a background in socioconstructivist analysis of instruction. The other has done work on realistic mathematics education (RME) that is carried out in the Netherlands.

The underlying philosophy of design research is that you have to understand the innovative forms of education that you might want to bring about in order to be able to produce them. This fits with the adage "if you want to change something, you have to understand it, and if you want to understand something, you have to change it." The two sides of this adage mirror the authors' histories. The socioconstructivist approach was inspired by a desire for understanding, the RME approach by a need for educational change.

If we take the first part of the adage, which calls for understanding, we may observe that the notion of design research has been around for a long time. Various forms of professional instructional design may be perceived as informal predecessors of design research. The recognition that instructional design often had an innovative character, while the available scientific knowledge base was far too limited to ground the design work sparked the idea for a type of instructional design that integrated design and research. This idea was strengthened by the experience that conscious and thorough instructional design work brought about a learning process in which the designers developed valuable and well-grounded knowledge in what retro-spectively might be called design experiments.

Over time a number of proposals have been made to define design research in mathematics education, of which Brown's (1992) article on design experi-ments is one of the most notable. In the Netherlands, Freudenthal *et al.* (1976) were perhaps the first to propose an approach of this type with the concept of "developmental research," an idea that was further elaborated by Streefland (1990) and Gravemeijer (1994, 1998).[2] Freudenthal's ideas were put to practice in the Dutch Institute for the Development of Mathematics Education (IOWO; which was later known as OW&OC and is now called Freudenthal Institute). This work has created fertile ground for the develop-ment of the so-called domain-specific instruction theory[3] of RME (Treffers 1987). This domain-specific theory can be reconstructed as a generalization over numerous local instruction theories (Gravemeijer 1994).

The second part of the adage, "if you want to understand something, you have to change it," points to the other predecessor of our collaborative work on design research, the constructivist "teaching experiment methodology" (Cobb and Steffe 1983; Steffe 1983). In this methodology, one-to-one teaching experiments aimed primarily at understanding how students learn rather than educational change. These one-to-one teaching experiments were later expanded into classroom teaching experiments. The need for classroom teaching experiments arose when analysis of traditional instruction within the same (socioconstructivist) research program produced only negative advice for the teachers; advice of the type: *Don't do this, don't do that.* To create more productive classroom environments, researchers had to take the responsibility for the design of classroom instruction for an extended period of time. In doing so, the one-on-one teaching experiment methodology was expanded to classroom teaching experiments.

The focus on understanding is a salient characteristic of design research. In this respect, the distinction Bruner (1994) makes between research that aims at (statistical) explanation, and research that aims at understanding comes to mind. We may use this distinction to emphasize that the goal of design research is very different from experimental or quasi-experimental research. And different goals imply different methods and different forms of justifica-tion. In relation to this we may quote the NCTM Research Advisory Committee (1996) that observes "a shift in norms of justification" in mathe-matics education research. The Committee argues that this is a shift from research that proves that treatment A works better than treatment B, towards research that has providing *an empirically grounded theory on how the inter-vention works* as its goal.

Note that the intended result of this type of research is theory. The purpose of design experiments is to develop theories about both the process of learning and the means designed to support that learning. One may work towards this goal in two ways, either by developing local instruction theories, or by developing theoretical frameworks that address more encompassing issues. In our approach to design research, we try to combine the two.

In the following, we define what design research is for us by discussing the three phases of conducting a design experiment: (1) preparing for the experiment, (2) experimenting in the classroom, and (3) conducting retrospective analyses. In so doing, we will address a range of methodological considerations. To ground the discussion in a concrete design experiment, we will use an experiment on statistics to illustrate the various phases. Although some may not consider statistics a part of mathematics, we contend that this illustrative case of statistics education is compatible with the kind of mathematics education we seek to bring about.

Phase one – preparing for the experiment

From a design perspective, the goal of the preliminary phase of a design research experiment is to formulate a local instruction theory that can be elaborated and refined while conducting the experiment. From a research perspective, a crucial issue is that of clarifying the study's theoretical intent. In elaborating these points, we will start by clarifying how one goes about establishing the learning goals, or instructional endpoints at which one is aiming, and the instructional starting points. Next, we will discuss the conjectured local instruction theory that the research team has to develop. This local instruction theory encompasses both provisional instructional activities, and a conjectured learning process that anticipates how students' thinking and understanding might evolve when the instructional activities are employed in the classroom. We will close this section by elaborating on the theoretical intent of an experiment.

Endpoints

The preparation for a classroom design experiment typically begins with the clarification of the mathematical learning goals. Such a clarification is needed, as one cannot simply adopt the educational goals that are current in a given domain. These goals will, in practice, largely be determined by history, tradition, and assessment practices. Design researchers therefore cannot just take these goals as a given when starting a design experiment. Instead, they will have to problematize the topic under consideration from a disciplinary perspective, and ask themselves: What are the core ideas in this domain?

We can illustrate this activity of problematizing with our work in the domain of early statistics.

> The conventional content of statistics at the US Middle School level (12–14-year-old students) is rather meager. It is basically a collection of

separate topics—such as mean, median, and mode—and standardized graphical representations. Reviewing the literature, however, did not offer much help, there appeared to be no consensus on what the central ideas should be. By analyzing what doing statistics entails, we came to the conclusion that the notion of distribution plays a central role. We concluded that distribution could function as an overarching idea that could go through elementary school, middle school, and up to high school and college. From this perspective, notions like "center", "skewness", "spread", and "relative frequency" are ways of characterizing how the data are distributed, rather than separate topics or concepts in themselves. In addition, different types of statistical representations come to the fore as different ways of structuring and organizing data sets in order to detect relevant patterns and trends.

This elaboration serves to emphasize that the goal of design research is not to take the currently instituted or institutionalized school curriculum as a given, and to try to find better ways to achieve the already defined goals. Instead, the research team has to scrutinize those goals from a disciplinary point of view in order to establish what the most relevant or useful goals are. Consequently, the design research we describe here is interventionist in character. In our example, part of our agenda was to attempt to influence what statistics should be in school, at least at a middle school level in the United States of America.

Starting points

In order to be able to develop a conjectured local instruction theory, one also has to consider the instructional starting points. Note that the focus in doing so is to understand the consequences of earlier instruction, not merely to document the typical level of reasoning of 12- or 14-year-old students in a given domain. Here, the existing research literature can be useful. Psychological studies can usually be interpreted as documenting the effects of prior instructional history. To complement such a literature study, the researchers will also have to carry out their own assessments before starting a design experiment. In some cases, they may be able to use available items and instruments. In addition to written tests, there will also be a need for other forms of assessment, such as interviews, or whole class performance assessments. We have found whole-class performance assessments to be particularly useful in documenting instructional starting points. We may illustrate this with the example of the statistics design experiment.

> In preparation for the design experiment in data analysis, we gave a number of tasks to two classes. Then, rather than attempting to support the students' learning in the whole class discussion, the role of the

teacher was to probe the students' understanding and reasoning, and to find out why they used particular approaches. These performance assessments clearly revealed the consequences of the students' prior instruction. For them, data analysis was trying to remember what you're supposed to do with numbers. Data were not numbers plus context for them, to use a phrase from Moore (1997). In his view, statisticians are always dealing with data plus context. In other words, data for these students were not measures of an attribute of a situation that was relevant with regard to the problem or issue under investigation. So, our initial challenge in the design experiment was to support a change in what statistics was about for these students, so that they were actually analyzing data.

Local instruction theory

Given the potential endpoints on the one hand and the instructional starting points on the other, the research team has to formulate a local instruction theory. Such a local instruction theory consists of conjectures about a possible learning process, together with conjectures about possible means of supporting that learning process. The means of support encompass potentially productive instructional activities and (computer) tools as well as an envisioned classroom culture and the proactive role of the teacher. The research team tries to anticipate how students' thinking and understanding might evolve when the planned but revisable instructional activities are used in the classroom. In this manner, the research team tries to reconcile the need to plan in advance with the need to be flexible when building on the students' current understanding when the design experiment is underway.

In many domains, the available research literature provides only limited guidance. In the case of statistics we had to work hard to find five relevant articles.[4] The sort of articles that are relevant for construing local instruction theories are reports of the process of students' learning in a particular domain together with descriptions of the instructional settings, the tasks, and the tools that enabled or supported that learning.

To compensate for the lack of guidance that the literature offers, design researchers have to turn to other resources, such as curricula, texts on mathematics education, and the like. Actually, the design researcher may take ideas from a variety of sources to construe an instructional sequence. Note, however, that adopting often means adapting. In this respect, the way of working of a design researcher resembles the manner of working of what the French call a *bricoleur* – an experienced tinker/handy person who uses, as much as possible, those materials that happen to be available. To do so, many materials will have to be adapted; the *bricoleur* may even have to invent new applications, which differ from what the materials were designed for. The design researcher follows a similar approach, labeled "theory-guided bricolage" (Gravemeijer 1994), to indicate that the way in which selections and adaptations are made will be guided by a (possibly still emergent) domain-specific instruction theory.

The classroom culture and the proactive role of the teacher

Instructional designers typically focus on instructional tasks and tools as potential means of support. We would argue, however, that one also has to consider the characteristics of the envisioned classroom culture and pro-active role of the teacher. One cannot plan instructional activities without considering how they are going to be enacted in the classroom. Design researchers therefore also have to consider the nature of classroom norms and the nature of classroom discourse. We know from experience that the norms of argumentation can differ radically from one classroom to another, and that they can make a profound difference in the nature and the quality of the students' mathematical learning (Cobb *et al.* 1989). Considerations on classroom norms and classroom discourse should therefore be included in the design.

One of the tasks of the teacher will be to establish the desired classroom culture. Furthermore, the proactive role of the teacher will include introducing the instructional activities, or more specifically in the case of statistics, guiding the process of talking through the data creation process. The teacher will also have to select possible topics for discussion, and orchestrate whole class discussions on these topics.

Theoretical intent

In addition to elaborating a preliminary instructional design, the research group also has to formulate the theoretical intent of the design experiment, because the goal of a design experiment is not just to describe what happened in a particular classroom. Analyses will have to define cases of more general phenomena that can inform design or teaching in other situations. One of the primary aims of a design experiment is to support the constitution of an empirically grounded local instruction theory.

Another aim of a design experiment might be to place classroom events in a broader context by framing them as instances of more encompassing issues. For example, analyses that focus on the proactive role of the teacher, teacher's and students' negotiation of general classroom norms, or the teacher's learning might be conducted. Also, the role of symbolizing and modeling, or more generally of semiotic processes, in supporting students' learning can become an explicit focus of investigation. The statistics design experiment became a case of cultivating students' mathematical interests in that in the course of these experiments students became very interested in conducting data analysis to investigate issues. They came to view this as an activity worthy of their engagement. This relates to issues such as motivation and persistence. Ultimately, this might influence their decision of whether or not to continue studying mathematics. For us, the cultivation of students' domain-specific interests is an important aspect of mathematical literacy in its own right.

In addition to these more encompassing issues, we may point to a third type of theory that could emerge during a series of design experiments. A series of design experiments can serve as the context for the development of theories or theoretical frameworks that entail new scientific categories that can do useful work in generating, selecting, and assessing design alternatives. The development of a conceptual framework to describe the phenomena under study is an essential part of a scientific endeavor. New categories, however, do not come ready-made, and cannot simply be captured by writing down a definition. New categories have to be invented and embedded in a supporting theoretical framework. Defining scientific terms is more like finding and validating a new category of existence in the world, for which we may use the term *ontological innovation* (diSessa and Cobb, 2004). Examples of such ontological innovations include the framework for interpreting classroom discourse and communication, which we will discuss later (Cobb and Yackel 1996), the discovery of metarepresentational competence (diSessa 1992, 2002), the theory of quantitative reasoning (Thompson and Thompson 1994, 1996), the design heuristic of emergent modeling (Gravemeijer 1999), and RME theory in general (Treffers 1987; Gravemeijer 1994). The new frameworks and categories may be sought after, but they often emerge from design experiments in answer to the need to get a handle on surprising observations. The initial conceptualization, however, will typically be crude and in need of further elaboration and improvement. Ontological innovations therefore become a topic of a research program that spans a series of design experiments, within which the theoretical frameworks will be revised and refined to adjust to a range of design contexts.

Mark that ontological innovations can play a dual role. On the one hand, they can serve as lenses for making sense of what is happening in the complex, more-or-less real world instructional setting in which a design study is conducted. On the other hand, ontological innovations can function as guidelines or heuristics for instructional design. The concepts of social norms and sociomathematical norms that we will discuss in more detail later, may function as an example. The concepts offer an interpretative framework for analyzing classroom discourse and communication. The same framework also reveals what norms to aim for to make the design experiment successful. RME theory may play a similar dual role; the theory not only guides the design, but also offers a framework for interpreting the students' learning process. One point of attention, for instance, will be the variety of solution procedures that the students produce. This can be seen as an indication of the extent to which these solution procedures are student inventions rather than regurgitated copies of examples given by the teacher or other students. Moreover, according to the reinvention principle, one expects the variation in solution procedures to correspond with the conjectured reinvention route.

Phase two – the design experiment

The second phase consists of actually conducting the design experiment. When all the preparation has been done, the overall endpoints are specified, the starting points defined, and a conjectured local instruction theory formulated, the design experiment can start. The research group will take the responsibility for the learning process of a group of students, whether it be for 5 weeks, for 3 months, or even for a whole school year. However, before describing this second phase, it is important to clarify the intent or purpose of actually experimenting in the classroom.

Although, for some, the term *experiment* may evoke associations with experimental, or quasi-experimental, research, the objective of the design experiment is not to try and demonstrate that the initial design or the initial local instruction theory works. The overall goal is not even to assess whether it works, although, of course, the researchers will necessarily do so. Instead, the purpose of the design experiment is both to test and improve the conjectured local instruction theory that was developed in the preliminary phase, and to develop an understanding of how it works.

We will start our discussion of the design experiment with the iterative sequence of tightly integrated cycles of design and analysis, which is key to the process of testing, improving, and understanding. Next, we will briefly touch upon the kind of data that are generated. Then, we address the need for explicating the interpretative framework(s) one uses for interpreting classroom discourse and communication as well as for interpreting students' mathematical reasoning and learning.

Microcycles of design and analysis

At the heart of the design experiment lies a cyclic process of (re)designing and testing instructional activities and other aspects of the design. In each lesson cycle, the research team conducts an anticipatory thought experiment by envisioning how the proposed instructional activities might be realized in interaction in the classroom, and what students might learn as they participate in them. During the enactment of the instructional activities in the classroom, and in retrospect, the research team tries to analyze the actual process of student participation and learning. On the basis of this analysis, the research team makes decisions about the validity of the conjectures that are embodied in the instructional activity, the establishment of particular

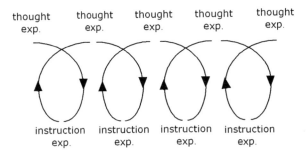

Figure 3.1 Developmental research, a cumulative cyclic process

norms, and the revision of those specific aspects of the design. The design experiment therefore consists of cyclic processes of thought experiments and instruction experiments (Freudenthal 1991; Figure 3.1).

We may associate these microcycles of design and analysis with Simon's (1995) "mathematical teaching cycle." According to this idea, a mathematics teacher will first try to anticipate what the mental activities of the students will be when they participate in some envisioned instructional activities. Then the teacher will try to find out to what extent the actual thinking processes of the students correspond with the hypothesized ones during the enactment of those activities to finally reconsider potential or revised follow-up activities. To characterize the teacher's thinking, Simon coined the term, "hypothetical learning trajectory," which he described as "The consideration of the learning goal, the learning activities, and the thinking and learning in which the students might engage" (Simon 1995: 133). The mathematical teaching cycle, then, may be described as conjecturing, enacting, and revising hypothetical learning trajectories.

We may compare the microcycles of design and analysis with the concept of an empirical cycle of hypotheses testing. A fundamental difference, however, is that the evaluation of the former concerns inferences about the mental activities of the students, not merely observable behavior of the students, since the goal for the design researcher is not just to find out whether the participation of the students in those particular activities results in certain anticipated behaviors, but to understand the relation between the students' participation and the conjectured mental activities.

To give an example of other such conjectures we may return to our example of statistics.

Earlier we stated that one of our initial goals was that the students would actually be analyzing data, not just numbers without context. With that in mind, we instituted a process that we called "talking through the

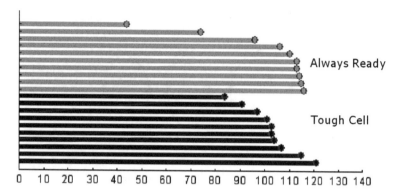

Figure 3.2   Two data sets in minitool 1

process of data creation." On the basis of pragmatic considerations, and since our focus was on data analysis, we did not involve the students in activities of data gathering. We did not, however, want the data to drop out of thin air for the students. Moreover, following Tzou (2000), we would argue that data are not ready available; data are created. Data are the result of measuring, and often specific measures are construed to find an answer to a certain question. We conjectured that it would be essential for students to experience this process of creating data to answer a question if data were to be measures rather than mere numbers for them. We may illustrate this with an example.

In one of the initial instructional activities, we wanted the students to compare data on the life span of two brands of batteries. However, it was important that they do so for a reason that they considered legitimate. The teacher therefore began by asking the students if they used batteries, and what they used them for. They told that they used them in portable CD-players, tape recorders, and so forth. So, for them the quality of batteries appeared to be a significant issue. Next the teacher asked about the things that they focus on when buying batteries. The students came up with life span and costs. So together teacher and students identified life span as a relevant dimension. Then the discussion turned to how to figure out which of two different brands of batteries would have the better life span. And the students were asked to come up with ideas about how to make measurements. They offered various proposals, often the idea came up of putting a number of batteries in "identical" appliances, everything from torch flash lights, to clocks, to whatever. It was only against that background of actually having talked through the data creation process that the data the students were to analyze were introduced. In doing so, we conjectured that as a consequence of engaging in this process the data that were introduced would have a history for the students. Shown in Figure 3.2 are the data on the life span of two brands of batteries, which are presented by "magnitude-value bars" in the first computer minitool.

Each bar signifies the life span of a single battery. This computer tool has a number of options; the students can for example sort the bars by size, by the colors that correspond with different subsets. When we introduced this type of visual representation, we purposely chose situations with linearity, such as time, that in our view would fit with this representation. We conjectured that this representation would be relatively transparent for the students thanks to their experience with scale lines and the like. We further conjectured that the students would focus on the position of the endpoints of the bars when comparing the data sets, and that the combination of a significant number of high values of the Always Ready batteries in combination with a few short life spans would create opportunities for a productive discussion.

In this example we focused on various conjectures, such as the conjecture that by engaging students in the task of comparing two sets of data, which differed markedly in distribution of data values – while using the first minitool – would lead to a discussion about how the data values are distributed. We would be remiss if we did not clarify that the actual conjectures were in fact more complex, in that they also encompassed choices about organization of the classroom activities and classroom norms, as well as the nature of instructional activities and tools. These are relatively detailed conjectures about the means of supporting shifts in students' reasoning that we anticipated would be important.

As a clarifying note, it is helpful to distinguish between two complementary ways of identifying causal relations – the regularity conception of causality that is connected to observed regularities, and a process-oriented conception of causal explanation "that sees causality as fundamentally referring to the actual causal mechanisms and processes that are involved in particular events and situations" (Maxwell 2004: 4). In the latter, a "causal explanation" of a causal relation refers to "the mechanisms through which and the conditions under which that causal relationship holds" (Shadish *et al.* (2002), cited in Maxwell (2004: 4)). In contrast to the regularity conception of causality, causal explanation can, in principle, be identified in a single case (Maxwell 2004: 6). These mechanisms are exactly the kind of causal explanation that the design researchers seek to develop. In this sense, the microcycles of thought and instruction experiments correspond to a process-oriented conception of causal explanation, while the empirical cycle corresponds with the regularity conception of causality. Note, however, that in the context of design research, it will not be sufficient to come to understand one student's thinking. Instead, to be of value, the researchers must document that a significant proportion of

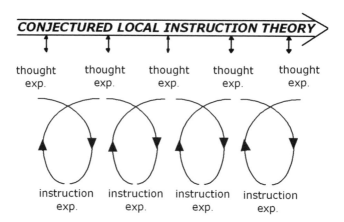

Figure 3.3   Reflexive relation between theory and experiments

students reason in a comparable manner. In addition, regularities in the variation in student thinking will be essential for productive classroom discussions.

In a design experiment, the microcycles of thought and instruction experiments serve the development of the local instruction theory. In fact, there is a
reflexive relation between the thought and instruction experiments and the
local instruction theory that is being developed. On one hand, the conjectured local instruction theory guides the thought and instruction experiments, and on the other, the microcycles of design and analysis shape the
local instruction theory (Figure 3.3).

These microcycles require that the research team engages in an ongoing
analysis of individual students' activity and of classroom social processes to
inform new anticipatory thought experiments, the design or revision of
instructional activities, and, sometimes, the modification of learning goals.
In service of such an analysis, it is critical in our experience that the
researchers are present in the classroom when the design experiment is
in progress, and conduct short debriefing sessions with the collaborating
teacher immediately after each classroom session in order to develop shared
interpretations of what might be going on in the classroom.

We also find it vital to have longer periodic meetings. The focus of these
meetings is primarily on the conjectured local instruction theory as a whole. A
local instruction theory encompasses both the overall process of learning and
the instructional activities that are designed to foster the mental activities that
constitute the long-term process. So, we may also observe a process of conjecturing and revising on two levels, on the level of the individual classroom
sessions, and on the level of the instructional sequence as a whole. In addition
to the adaptation of the overall learning process during a design experiment,
we may also discern macrocycles, which span entire experiments, in the sense

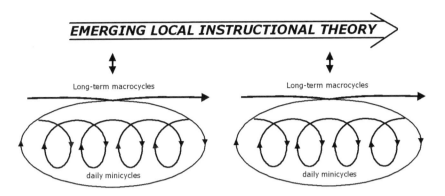

Figure 3.4   Micro- and macro-design cycles

that the retrospective analysis of a design experiment can feed forward to inform a subsequent experiment (Figure 3.4). From this process emerges a more robust local instructional theory that, we would add, is still potentially revisable.

Data generation

Decisions about the types of data that need to be generated in the course of an experiment depend on the theoretical intent of the design experiment. These are in a sense pragmatic decisions in that the data have to make it possible for researchers to address the issues that were identified as the theoretical intent at the start of the design experiment. If the design experiment focuses on the development of a local instruction theory, for instance, it makes sense to video record all classroom sessions, conduct pre- and post-interviews with the students, make copies of all of the students' work, and assemble field notes. In addition, appropriate benchmark assessment items that have been used by other researchers might be incorporated if they are available.

We also find it crucial to audio record the regular research group meetings because these meetings offer one of the best opportunities to document the learning process of the research team. Data generation therefore involves keeping a log of the ongoing interpretations, conjectures, and decisions.

The specific foci of a design experiment may require additional types of data. For an illustration, we return to the statistics experiment again, which also became a case of cultivating students' mathematical interests (Cobb and Hodge 2003). We were therefore interested in how the students perceived their obligations in the classroom and how they evaluated those obligations. As a consequence, a member of the research team conducted student interviews that focused on these issues while the experiment was in progress. It turned out to be more productive to conduct these interviews with pairs or groups of three students. So, this specific research interest necessitated another form of data collection.

Interpretative framework(s)

A key element in the ongoing process of experimentation is the interpretation of both the students' reasoning and learning and the means by which that learning is supported and organized. We contend that it is important to be explicit about how one is going about interpreting what is going on in the classroom.

In (quasi-)experimental research, the relation between empirical reality and scientific interpretation is made explicit by operationalizing the variables that are taken into account. Likewise, design researchers have to explicate how they translate observations of events in the classroom into scientific interpretations. The researchers will necessarily employ an interpretive framework to make sense of the complexity and messiness of classroom events while a design experiment is in progress as well as when conducting a retrospective analysis of the data generated during an experiment. It is essential in our view that researchers explicate the basic constructs of their interpretive framework if inquiry is to be disciplined and systematic. Key elements of such a (potentially revisable) interpretative framework include (1) a framework for interpreting the evolving classroom learning environment, and (2) a framework for interpreting student mathematical reasoning and learning mathematics. In the following we will first discuss the framework we use to interpret classroom discourse and communication, and next turn to the domain-specific instruction theory for realistic mathematics education that is used as a conceptual framework for interpreting student learning. In doing so, we clarify that, for us, socioconstructivism functions as a background theory.

Emergent perspective

The framework that we currently use for interpreting classroom discourse and communication is the *emergent perspective* (Cobb and Yackel 1996; Yackel and Cobb 1996; Figure 3.5). We mentioned aspects of this framework earlier as examples of an ontological innovation.

The framework can be viewed as a response to the issue of attempting to understand mathematical learning as it occurs in the social context of the classroom. With regard to the specifics of the framework, the column headings *Social Perspective* and *Psychological Perspective* involve a focus on the classroom community and on individual students' reasoning, respectively. In the following paragraphs, we first discuss social norms, then sociomathematical norms, and finally classroom mathematical practices.

Social norms refer to expected ways of acting and explaining that become

Social Perspective	Psychological Perspective
Classroom social norms	Beliefs about our own role, others' roles, and the general nature of mathematical activity
Socio-mathematical norms	Specifically mathematical beliefs and values
Classroom mathematical practices	Mathematical conceptions and activity

Figure 3.5   An interpretive framework for analyzing individual and collective activity at the classroom level

established through a process of mutual negotiation between the teacher and students. The social norms will differ significantly between classrooms that pursue traditional mathematics, and those that engage in reform mathematics. In traditional mathematics classrooms, the role of the teacher is to explain and evaluate, while the social norms include the obligation of the students to try to figure out what the teacher has in mind, and act accordingly. Examples of norms for whole class discussions in reform math classrooms include obligations for the students to explain and justify solutions, attempt to make sense of explanations given by others, indicate agreement and disagreement, and question alternatives in situations where a conflict in interpretations or solutions is apparent.

The psychological correlate to social norms concerns the teacher's and students' individual beliefs about their own and others' roles. The reflexivity between social norms and individual beliefs is better understood when analyzing the negotiation process of classroom communities. On the one hand, an individual's beliefs about ways to act contribute to the negotiation of social norms. On the other hand, an individual's beliefs are enabled and constrained as he or she participates in this negotiation process.

The *sociomathematical norms* can be distinguished from social norms as ways of explicating and acting in whole class discussions that are specific to mathematics. Examples of such sociomathematical norms include what counts as a different mathematical solution, a sophisticated mathematical solution, an efficient mathematical solution, and an acceptable mathematical explanation and justification. The students' personal beliefs about what makes a contribution acceptable, different, sophisticated or efficient encompass the psychological correlate of the sociomathematical norms. Students develop personal ways of judging whether a solution is efficient or different, and these beliefs are mutually negotiated as the classroom microculture is continually being structured. That is, the teacher cannot merely state specific guidelines for what types of solutions are acceptable and expect the guidelines to be understood and enacted by students. Instead, sociomathematical norms are continually negotiated and redefined as the teacher and students participate in discussions.

The analysis of sociomathematical norms has proved to be pragmatically significant when conducting design experiments in that it clarifies the process by which teachers may foster the development of intellectual autonomy in their classrooms. To create the opportunity for the students to take over the teacher's responsibility as validators, sociomathematical norms that enable students to make independent judgments that contribute to the teacher's teaching agenda have to be in place.

The last social aspect of the theoretical framework concerns the *mathematical practices* that are established in the classroom (Cobb *et al.* 2001). A mathematical practice can be described as the normative ways of acting, communicating and symbolizing mathematically at a given moment in time. In contrast to sociomathematical norms that are specific to mathematics, mathematical practices are specific to particular mathematical ideas or concepts. In addition, mathematical practices necessarily evolve in the course of an experiment whereas sociomathematical norms tend to be more stable. An indication that a certain mathematical practice has been established is that explanations pertaining to it have gone beyond justification. Individual students' mathematical interpretations and actions constitute the psychological correlates of classroom mathematical practices. Their interpretations and the mathematical practices are reflexively related in that students' mathematical development occurs as they contribute to the constitution of mathematical practices. Conversely, the evolution of mathematical practices does not occur apart from students' reorganization of their individual activities.

We may conclude by noting that in the context of a design experiment, a detailed analysis of evolving classroom practices offers a way of describing the actual learning process of the classroom community as a whole. This offers a viable alternative for describing the learning process of the classroom rather than implying that all students are learning in unison, or attempting to describe the learning processes of each individual student.

RME theory

When discussing theoretical intent of design experiments, we noted that ontological innovations, such as interpretative frameworks, serve a dual role both as lenses for making sense of what is happening in a real-world instructional setting, and as guidelines or heuristics for instructional design. On the one hand, we may observe that although the emergent framework was initially developed to interpret classroom discourse and communication, it also offers guidelines on classroom culture characteristics that fit the intended learning ecology. On the other hand, it may be observed that the RME theory not only offers design heuristics, but may also function as an framework for interpreting student activity in terms of learning mathematics.

In the following we elaborate this dual role of RME theory. Given its origin, we focus first on the instructional design perspective.

RME emerged at least in part in resistance to instructional and design approaches that treated mathematics as a ready-made product. Freudenthal (1971, 1973) argued that mathematics should primarily have the character of an activity for the students. A process of guided reinvention then would have to ensure that this mathematical activity would foster the construal of mathematics as a body of knowledge by the students. This requires the instructional starting points to be experientially real for the students, which means that one has to present the students with problem situations in which they can reason and act in a personally meaningful manner. The objective of guided reinvention is that the mathematics that the students develop will also be experientially real for them. Learning mathematics should ideally be experienced as expanding one's mathematical reality.

We may further elaborate this point by clarifying the way in which Freudenthal (1991: 17) conceives reality, "I prefer to apply the term reality to what common sense experiences as real at a certain stage". He goes on to say that reality is to be understood as a mixture of interpretation and sensual experience, which implies that mathematics, too, can become part of a person's reality. Reality and what a person perceives as common sense is not static but grows, and is affected by the individual's learning process. The goal of realistic mathematics education then is to support students in creating a new mathematical reality. This is to be realized by guided reinvention, or *progressive mathematization* – if we take a student perspective. Progressive mathematization refers to a mixture of two forms of mathematizing, horizontally and vertically, which refers respectively to students mathematizing subject matter from reality, or mathematizing their own mathematical activity (Treffers 1987). This latter activity is essential in the constitution of a new mathematical reality, as "The activity on one level is subjected to analysis on the next, the operational matter on one level becomes subject matter on the next level" (Freudenthal 1971: 417). This shift from "activity" to "subject matter" relates to the shift from procedures to objects, which Sfard (1991) observed in the history of mathematics.

If we look at the history of mathematics, we may observe that mathematics emerged from solving problems, or as Freudenthal puts it, from organizing subject matter. According to Freudenthal (1983), mathematical "thought-things," such as concepts, tools and procedures, are invented to organize certain phenomena. The reinvention heuristic then suggests that the instructional designer should try to find situations that create the need for the

students to invent the mathematical thought-things the students are supposed to construct. To find such situations, the instructional designer should
analyze the relation between those mathematical thought-things, and the
phenomena they organize. This analysis lays the basis for a didactical
phenomenology (Freudenthal 1983), which also incorporates a discussion of
what phenomenological analysis means from an educational perspective. For
example, to construct distribution as a mathematical object, students should
be confronted with situations where it is reasonable and sensible for them to
achieve a goal by organizing phenomena in terms of distributions.

Freudenthal's level theory also shaped the RME view on educational
models. Instead of ready-made models, RME looks for models that may
emerge first as *models of* situated activity, and then gradually evolve into
entities of their own to function as *models for* more sophisticated mathematical reasoning (Gravemeijer 1999). According to this *emergent-modeling*
heuristic, the model and the new mathematical reality co-evolve; the emergence of the model is reflexively related to the development of some new
mathematical reality. The teacher may aid this process by supporting a shift
in the students' attention from the context that the model refers to, towards
the mathematical relations involved. In this manner, the students may
develop a network of mathematical relations. Then the model can begin to
function as a model for more sophisticated mathematical reasoning, in that
the model derives its meaning from this network of mathematical relations.
At the same time, relations in this network may themselves become mathematical objects that constitute a new mathematical reality. As a further elucidation, we may note that, the term *model* should not be taken too literally in
that it can also concern a model situation, or a model procedure. Moreover,
what is taken as *the model* from a more overarching design perspective will
be constituted as a series of submodels in the instructional activities.

As we argued before, the RME domain-specific instruction theory also
offers a framework for interpreting student activity in terms of learning mathematics (Gravemeijer 1994). It orients the researcher to focus, for instance, on
the various learning processes that might take place, with a special attention to
the question of whether the students are inventing their own solution procedures or are merely imitating the teacher or some leading students. In such a
case, one might look at the variety of students' solution procedures. On the
basis of the reinvention principle, one would further expect to recognize the
reinvention route in the students' solutions. In addition, one would expect that
the students would spontaneously drop back in their collective learning
history when they are faced with new problems that represent difficulties for
them. If they instead choose informal procedures that do not correspond with
the reinvention route that has been followed, this would be an indication that
that route is not experienced as a natural reinvention process.

In a similar manner, the researcher may investigate whether the models
that are used fit with the informal solution procedures demonstrated by the

students: Do the students use similar procedures with the model, as they did (or would do) without the model? In other words, the model must not dictate to the students how to proceed, but must be a resource that fits with their thought processes (Gravemeijer 1993). Along these lines, the RME framework might generate additional points of focus, such as the following

- Do the students rely on their own domain-specific knowledge?
- Do the instructional activities provide the expected traction for the students' informal solution procedures?
- Do the solutions that the students develop offer possibilities for vertical mathematization?
- Do the students mathematize their own informal mathematical activities?

and so forth. We will not try to be exhaustive here.

We want to close this section on the second phase of the design experiment methodology by presenting a short sketch of the instructional sequence that was developed in the statistics design experiment.

> We clarified the set up of the statistics sequence by first describing how the didactic phenomenological analysis plays out in this case. The first step in this analysis was to analyze the notion of distribution as a mathematical (or statistical) thought-thing. This led to the conclusion that distribution can be thought of as a density function, indicating that density can be conceived of as that which is organized by distribution as a thought-thing. Density – as a thought-thing in and of itself – in turn organizes collections of data points in a space of possible data values. This insight can be made concrete as a dot plot, showing data points on an axis (for example, these data points on an axis can be viewed as thought-things that organize data values). The measures can in turn be thought of as a means for getting a handle on some real world phenomena; the notion of data creation can also be construed as a form of organizing.
>
> This phenomenological analysis reveals a possible reinvention route in which a cumulative process of organizing would lead the students through the above steps in reverse order. This lays the basis for the following instructional sequence.
>
> Point of departure is a bottom-up approach in which students view the computer minitools as sensible tools to use, given their current conceptions of analyzing data. So, for the students, the primary function of the minitools is to help structure and describe data sets in order to make a decision or judgment. In this process, notions such as mean, mode, median, skewness, spreadoutness, and relative frequency may emerge as ways of describing how specific data sets are distributed within this space of values. Further, in this approach, various statistical representations or inscriptions may

emerge as different ways of structuring distributions. In fact, the minitools are so designed that they can support a process of progressive mathematization by which these conventional statistical tools are reinvented.

At the same time, the activity of structuring data sets using the minitools fosters a process by which the students come to view data sets as entities that are distributed within a space of possible values. The intent is to support a process in which the means of symbolizing, and the meaning of what these symbols signify for the students co-evolve, in a manner similar to that which Meira (1995: 270) describes when he speaks of a "dialectical relation between notations-in-use and mathematical sense making" (Meira 1995: 270).

The backbone of the sequence consists of a series of inscriptions that are embedded in the computer tools. The idea is that the activities with the computer tools succeed each other in such a manner that the activity with the newer tool is experienced as a natural extension of the activity with the earlier tool. The starting point is in the measures, or magnitudes, that constitute a data set. With the first minitool, magnitude-value bars (Figure 3.5) are introduced where each value bar signifies a single measure. (Initially, the measures under investigation are of a linear type, like length, and time. Later, this is generalized to other types of measures.) We conjectured that as a consequence of participating in discussions about various data sets represented by value bars, the students would begin to focus on the endpoints of value bars. As a consequence, these endpoints come to signify the corresponding value bars. This allows for the introduction of a line plot as a more condensed inscription that omits the value bars and preserves only the endpoints (Figure 3.6). The second minitool offers students a range of options for structuring data sets represented as line plots that include creating equal intervals, creating two equal groups, and creating four equal groups of data points. We conjectured that as a result of analyzing data sets using these options, the students would begin to reason about data in terms of density, and come to see the shape of the line plot as signifying the distribution of data values in terms of density.

In retrospect, we may recognize the emergent-modeling design heuristic

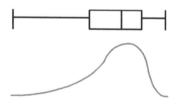

Figure 3.6   Box plot as a model for reasoning about distributions

with *a graphical representation of the shape of a distribution* as the over-arching model. This overarching model is instantiated by various sub-models that change over time. The graph was initially introduced in an informal manner, as a way of inscribing a set of measures by representing each measure by a bar (Figure 3.2). We can see this as a pre-stage of the model, where the set of measures is still very much tied to the situation. Nonetheless, from a statistical perspective, the shape of the distribution is visible in the way the endpoints are distributed in regard to the axis. In this phase, we can speak of the graphical representation as a *model of* a set of measures. Next, we introduced activities that were designed to draw the students' attention to distribution of the endpoints of the bars. This sup-ported the introduction of the line plot, where the second minitool was used to structure data sets in various ways to answer the questions at hand. Analyses that involved structuring the data into four equal groups with the corresponding tool option (which anticipates the box plot) were particularly important in drawing the students' attention to distribution of density. This then supported a gradual shift from seeing the graph as signifying a set of measures to seeing it as signifying a distribution. Once this latter shift occurred, the graph could then be used to reason about distributions. Students could, for instance, discern various types of distribu-tions (with the normal distributions as one of them), and could reason about characteristics of (univariate) distributions, like skewness (Figure 3.6). The model then became a *model for* reasoning about distributions.

Phase three – the retrospective analysis

Thus far, we have discussed the planning of a design experiment and the ongoing experimentation in the classroom that is central to the method-ology. A further aspect of the methodology concerns the retrospective analyses that are conducted of the entire data set collected during the experi-ment. The goal of the retrospective analyses will, of course, depend on the theoretical intent of the design experiment. However, one of the primary aims is typically to contribute to the development of a local instruction theory. Other goals may concern more encompassing issues, or ontological innovations. Although differences in theoretical objectives are reflected in differences in the retrospective analyses, the form of the analysis will neces-sarily involve an iterative process of analyzing the entire data set. We will, therefore, first describe the retrospective analyses in general, and then discuss analyses to develop a local instruction theory, and finally describe analyses conducted to address more general research topics.

The data sets typically include (but are not limited to) videotapes of all class-room lessons, video-recorded individual interviews conducted with all students before and after the experiment to assess their mathematical learning, copies of all the students' written work, field notes, and audio tapes of both the daily debriefing session and weekly project meetings. The challenge then is to analyze this comprehensive data set systematically while simultaneously documenting the grounds for particular inferences. Claims will be based on a retrospective, systematic and thorough analysis of the entire data set collected during the experiment. To ascertain the credibility of the analysis, all phases of the analysis process have to be documented, including the refining and refuting of conjectures. Final claims and assertions can then be justified by backtracking through the various levels of the analysis, if necessary to the original videotapes and transcripts. It is this documentation of the research team's learning process that provides an empirical grounding for analysis. Furthermore, it provides a means of differentiating systematic analyses in which sample episodes are used to illustrate general assertions from questionable analyses in which a few possibly atypical episodes are used to support unsubstantiated claims. Additional criteria that enhance the trustworthiness of an analysis include both the extent to which it has been critiqued by other researchers who do not have a stake in the success of the experiment and the extent to which it derives from a prolonged engagement with students and teachers (Taylor and Bogdan 1984). This latter criterion is typically satisfied in the case of classroom design experiments and constitutes the strength of the methodology.

The specific approach we use is a variant of Glaser and Strauss's (1967) constant comparative method (see also Cobb and Whitenack (1996)). We first work through the data chronologically, episode by episode, and at each point we test our current conjectures against the next episode. For example, one of the key criteria when we claim that a particular norm of argumentation has been established is that a student who appears to violate that norm will be critiqued by his or her classmates. If we find instances where such challenges do not occur, we either have to revise our conjecture about the norms of argumentation that have been established, or we have to substantiate the argument that the norms have evolved.

As a result of this first round of data analysis, we end up with a sequence of conjectures and refutations that are tied to specific episodes. In the second phase of a retrospective analysis, this sequence of conjectures and refutations in effect becomes the data. It is while *meta-analyzing* these episode-specific conjectures, confirmations and refutations, that particular episodes reveal themselves to be pivotal. And they are pivotal in the context of the analysis, because they allow us to decide between two or more competing conjectures. These are the episodes that are typically included in research reports. As an illustration, we present some typical episodes from the statistics design experiment.

> We already described the battery lifespan problem in which the data were represented as magnitude bars in the first computer tool. The students first worked on this problem in groups, and then the teacher initiated a

whole class discussion of the students' analyses. The computer tool was projected on an overhead screen, the data were sorted by size, and the so-called "range tool" option was used to highlight the ten highest data values (see Figure 3.7).

One of the students, Casey, argued that the green batteries were better because seven of the top ten were green (Always Ready), and her argument is supported by another student.

JANICE: She's saying that out of ten of the batteries that lasted the longest, seven of them are green, and that's the most number, so the Always Ready batteries are better because more of those batteries lasted longer.

However, this argument was challenged by another student, James, who argued that four of the pink bars (Tough Cell) were "almost in that area and then if you put all those in you would have seven (rather than three pinks)."

Later in the discussion, Brad asked for the value tool (the single vertical line) to be placed at 80, in order to substantiate his claim that the Tough Cell brand is better.

BRAD: See, there's still green ones (Always Ready) behind 80, but all of the Tough Cell is above 80. I would rather have a consistent battery that I know will get me over 80 hours than one that you just try to guess.

One of the issues of interest in this episode is the use of the word *consistent*, which the students introduce as an informal way of describing the extent to which data sets were bunched up or spread out. This episode also proved to be pivotal in documenting that a norm of argumentation was being established, namely that students were obliged to explain why the way they had partitioned or organized or structured the data gave

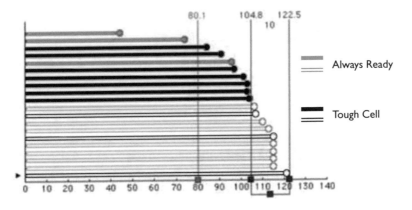

Figure 3.7 Battery life span data, Always Ready and Tough Cell batteries

insight into the problem or issue under investigation. We were able to demonstrate that this norm remained stable throughout the experiment.

A second illustrative episode concerns a comparison of two sets of data that showed the speeds of cars before and after a campaign against speeding (Figure 3.8).

In this case, one of the students had focused on the shape of the data sets to compare how they were distributed.

JANICE: If you look at the graphs and look at them like hills, then for the before group the speeds are spread out and more than 55, and if you look at the after graph, then more people are bunched up close to the speed limit which means that the majority of the people slowed down close to the speed limit.

What is of interest here is that this student did not use the word "hill" to refer to the figural image, but instead used it as a metaphor to describe the distribution of the density of the data ("bunched up close") as giving her insight into the effectiveness of the campaign against speeding. The students continued to use this metaphor throughout the design experiment to indicate that the "majority" of the data points were "bunched up." In a follow-up experiment, we found that the students could even identify where the hill was in the value-bar representation of the first computer minitool (Bakker 2004) – which underscores the metaphorical character of this term.

As a third example we may describe an episode in which the students had to compare data on T-cell counts for two different treatments for AIDS-patients, an experimental treatment with 46 patients, and a standard treatment with 186, where the goal is to raise the patients' T-cell counts.

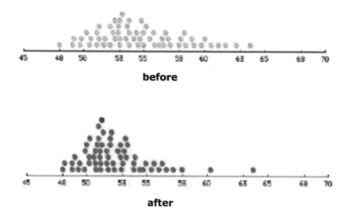

Figure 3.8   Speed data, before and after a speed campaign

Various groups of students analyzed these data in a range of different ways. One group of students identified the intervals where the "hill" was located in each data set, where the data were bunched up. And on this basis they argued that the new, experimental treatment was effective, because the "hill" was in a higher interval than the hill in the standard treatment data. Another group of students had used the four-equal-groups option (Figure 3.9).

This is a precursor of the box plot in that each interval contains 25% of the data. They had used another available option to hide the dots. Their argument was: the new treatment is better because 75% of the data is above 550, whereas in the traditional treatment 75% is below. Note that we could picture the shape of the hill in this representation, if we knew this was a uni-modal distribution.

We may briefly show why this notion of shape of a univariate distribution became important for analyzing bi-variate data in a subsequent design experiment conducted the following school year with some of the same students. In this follow-up experiment, we asked the students to compare, for instance, data on years of education, against salary levels for men, and women. The students analyzed data of this type by using a third computer minitool (Figure 3.10, left). One of the tool options was similar to the four-equal-groups option, rotated 90 degrees (Figure 3.10, right).

Here in doing so, the students typically talked about where the "hill" was located or where the "clutter" was in the data. As the students discovered, the ranges were similar for the men's and women's salary levels. The big difference was that the data for females was skewed much more heavily towards the bottom end of the distribution for each level of education. As this example clarifies, analyzing bi-variate data is not so much about

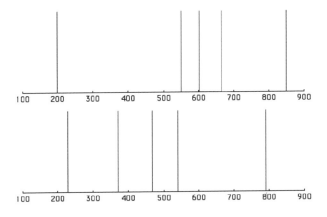

Figure 3.9 T-cell data, four-equal-groups inscription, with data points hidden

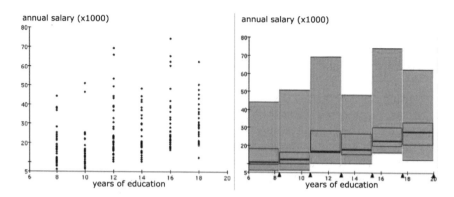

Figure 3.10 Salary against years of education

drawing a line through a cloud of dots, but about investigating how the distribution of the dependent variable changes as the independent variable changes.

Reconstructing the local instruction theory

One of the primary aims of a retrospective analysis is to support the constitution of a revised local instruction theory. However, it is important to emphasize that the results of design experiments cannot be linked to pre- and post-test results in the same direct manner as is common in standard formative evaluation because the proposed local instruction theory and prototypical instructional sequence will differ from those that are tried out in the classroom. Because of the testing and revising of conjectures while the experiment is in progress, a revised, potentially optimal instructional sequence has to be discerned by conducting a retrospective analysis. It does not make sense, for example, to include instructional activities that did not live up to the expectations of the researcher, but the fact that these activities were enacted in the experiment will nonetheless have affected the students' learning. Adaptations will therefore have to be made when the non-, or less-functional activities are left out. Consequently, the instructional sequence will be put together by focusing on and reconstructing the instructional activities that proved to constitute the effective elements of the sequence. This reconstruction of an optimal sequence will be based on the observations and inferences made during the design experiment, complemented by the insights gained by conducting retrospective analyses. In this manner, it can be claimed that the results of a design experiment are empirically grounded.

As a point of clarification we would like to add that, although the constitution of a revised local instruction theory is primarily a reconstruction activity, the retrospective analysis may spark design ideas that go beyond those that were tried out in the classroom. These insights might in turn create the need for a new experiment, starting with a new conjectured local instruction theory. Here, the cyclic nature of the methodology that we noted at the level of instructional design microcycles reappears at a broader level. An entire design experiment and the subsequent retrospective analysis together constitute a larger, macrocycle of design and analysis (Figure 3.4).

In this cycle, the conjectures and assumptions formulated at the outset when planning a design experiment are scrutinized in the retrospective analysis. An example of such an analysis can be found in Cobb *et al.* (1997). Here, the retrospective analysis indicated that several key assumptions that underpinned an instructional sequence were ill-founded. As a consequence, the instructional sequence was radically revised and a further design experiment was conducted. An extensive report of this largely successful follow-up experiment can be found in Stephan *et al.* (2003).

Encompassing issues and ontological innovations

In addition to retrospective analyses that directly aim at the reconstruction and revision of a local instructional theory, a retrospective analysis might be conducted to place classroom events in a broader context by framing them as instances of more encompassing issues. Earlier, we discussed analyses that focus on the role of the teacher, teacher's learning, semiotic processes, or on the process of cultivating the students' mathematical interests. In addition, we mentioned ontological innovations, which might include issues such as the framework for interpreting classroom discourse and communication, metarepresentational competence, quantitative reasoning or emergent modeling.

In such cases, the aim of the analysis is to frame events that occurred in the design experiment classroom as instances, or paradigm cases, of a broader class of phenomena. The goal is to come to understand (the role of) the specific characteristics of the investigated learning ecology in order to develop theoretical tools that make it possible to come to grips with the same phenomenon in other learning ecologies. Data analysis that aims at understanding a paradigm case differs significantly from data analyses that aim at establishing causal relations within a regularity conception of causality. Claims are not based on statistical analysis, but on a systematic and thorough analysis of the data set.

Virtual replicability

Metaphorically speaking, the course of a design experiment can be characterized in terms of the learning process of the research team. We would argue that this learning process has to justify the products of the research project. This characterization is especially fitting for the construal of the local instruction theory, which encompasses two processes, (1) the learning process that is inherent to the cyclic process of (re)designing and testing instructional activities and other aspects of the initial design, and (2) the retrospective analysis that scrutinizes, and builds on, this primary process, and looks for patterns that may explain the progress of the students. In relation to this learning process, we can refer to the methodological norm of "trackability" that is used as a criterion in ethnographic research. Smaling (1990, 1992) connects trackability with the well-known criterion of "reliability." He notes that reliability refers to the absence of accidental errors and is often defined as reproducibility. He goes on to say, that for qualitative research this means virtual replicability. Here, the emphasis is on virtual. It is important that the research is reported in such a manner that it can be retraced, or virtually replicated by other researchers. This ethnographic norm of trackability fits with Freudenthal's conception of developmental or design research:

> [D]evelopmental research means:
> experiencing the cyclic process of development and research so consciously, and reporting on it so candidly that it justifies itself, and this experience can be transmitted to others to become like their own experience.
>
> (Freudenthal 1991: 161)

Likewise, Smaling (1990: 6) states that trackability can be established by reporting on "failures and successes, on the procedures followed, on the conceptual framework and on the reasons for the choices made." Note that this norm of trackability does not necessarily require that everyone has to subscribe the conclusions of the researchers. Eventually, outsiders, who have virtually replicated the learning process of the researchers, may interpret their experiences differently or come to different conclusions on the same experiential basis. The power of this approach is that it creates an experiential basis for discussion.

Ecological validity

A central assumption that underpins our work is that instructional innovations developed in the course of a design research experiment can be used productively to support students' learning in other classrooms. However, as we know only too well, the history of research in education in general, and in mathematics education in particular, is replete with more than its share of disparate and often irreconcilable findings. A primary source of difficulty is that the independent variables of traditional experimental research are often relatively superficial and have little to do with either context or meaning. As a consequence, it has frequently been impossible to account for differences in findings when different groups of students supposedly receive the same instructional treatment.

In contrast to traditional experimental research, the challenge when conducting design experiments is not that of replicating instructional innovations by ensuring that they are realized in precisely the same way in different classrooms. The conception of teachers as professionals who continually adjust their plans on the basis of ongoing assessments of their students' mathematical understanding suggests, in fact, that complete replicability is neither desirable nor, perhaps, possible (Ball 1993; Simon 1995). Design research aims for ecological validity, that is to say, (the description of) the results should provide a basis for adaptation to other situations. The premise is that an empirically grounded theory of how the intervention works accommodates this requirement. Therefore, one of the primary aims of this type of research is not to develop the instructional sequence as such, but to support the constitution of an empirically grounded local instruction theory that underpins that instructional sequence. The intent is to develop a local instruction theory that can function as a frame of reference for teachers who want to adapt the corresponding instructional sequence to their own classrooms, and their personal objectives. One element that can be helpful in this respect is offering a *thick description* of what happened in the design experiment. By describing details of the participating students, of the teaching–learning process, and so forth, together with an analysis of how these elements may have influenced the whole process, outsiders will have a basis for deliberating adjustments to other situations. Conversely, feedback from teachers on how the instructional sequence was adjusted to accommodate various classrooms can strengthen the ecological validity significantly. We therefore find it critical to have repeated trials in a variety of settings.

In the case of the statistics sequence, for example, we worked with middle school students, with "at risk" high school students, prospective elementary teachers, practicing teachers, and there have also been follow-up groups, including a series of design experiments by Arthur Bakker (2004), in the Netherlands. We have been surprised by the extent to which we have been able to document regularities in the development of the participants' thinking across these various settings. That is to say, there is diversity in how a group of participants reasoned at any point in time. But we were able to predict with some confidence the primary types of analyses or forms of reasoning within a group at any point in the experiment. We think that is useful knowledge from a teacher's point of view in that it enables teachers to anticipate the types of reasoning that they can build on or work with.

Developing domain-specific instruction theories

Design research provides a means of developing local instruction theories that can serve as support for teachers who adapt instructional sequences as part of their teaching practice. In addition, design research also contributes to the development of a domain-specific instruction theory, in our case the RME theory. This theory emerges in an iterative, cumulative process that embraces a series of design research projects. In this regard, we can speak of theory development at various levels:

- the instructional activities (microtheories) level
- the instructional sequence (local instruction theories) level
- the domain-specific instruction theory level.

The relations between these levels can be clarified by drawing on the distinction that Kessels and Korthagen (1996) make between *episteme* and *phronesis*. Following Aristotle, they use the Greek word *episteme* to refer to scientific knowledge, and the word *phronesis* to refer to "practical wisdom." They argue that the incompatibility of the products of scientific research with the needs of teachers can be traced to the contrast between these two realms. Teachers rely on practical wisdom, which they share with one another in the form of narratives. They experience scientific knowledge produced by research as too abstract and general to directly inform their practice (see also Hiebert and Stigler 1999). In this respect, we would argue that design research has the potential to bridge the gap between theory and practice, as domain-specific instruction theory can be categorized as *episteme* and microdidactic theories as *phronesis*. In design research, scientific knowledge is grounded in practical wisdom while simultaneously providing heuristics that can strengthen practical wisdom.

Developing ways of analyzing innovations

A related challenge is that of developing ways of analyzing innovations that make their realization in different classrooms commensurable. An analysis of classroom events structured in terms of constructs such as social norms, sociomathematical norms, and classroom mathematical practices serves to relate the students' mathematical learning in a particular classroom to their participation in sequences of instructional activities as they were realized in that classroom. As we noted earlier, classroom social norms, and sociomath norms can make a profound difference in the nature and the quality of the students' mathematical reasoning.

This part of the retrospective analysis raises its own methodological issues. A theoretical analysis is the result of a complex, purposeful problem-solving process. One would therefore not expect that different researchers would necessarily develop identical theoretical constructs when analyzing the same set of design experiment data. This implies that the notion of replicability is not relevant in this context. Following Atkinson *et al.* (1988), we suggest that the relevant criteria are instead those of generalizability and the trustworthiness of the constructs developed.

We touched on the issue of generalizability when discussing the importance of viewing classroom events as paradigm cases of more encompassing issues. It is this framing of classroom activities and events as exemplars or prototypes that gives rise to generalizability. This, of course, is not generalization in the sense that the characteristics of particular cases are ignored and they are treated as interchangeable instances of the set to which assertions are claimed to apply. Instead, the theoretical analysis developed when coming to understand one case is deemed to be relevant when interpreting other cases. Thus, what is generalized is a way of interpreting and understanding specific cases that preserves their individual characteristics. For example, we conjectured that much of what we learned when investigating symbolizing and modeling in a first-grade design experiment that focused on arithmetical reasoning would inform analyses of other students' mathematical learning in a wide range of classroom situations including those that involve the intensive use of technology. This, in fact, proved to be the case in recently completed sequences of design experiments that focused on the students' development of statistical reasoning (Cobb 1999; Cobb *et al.* 2003). It is this quest for generalizability that distinguishes analyses whose primary goal is to assess a particular instructional innovation from those whose goal is the development of theory that can feed forward to guide future research and instructional design.

Whereas generalizability is closely associated with the notion of a paradigm case, trustworthiness is concerned with the reasonableness and justifiability of inferences and assertions. This notion of trustworthiness acknowledges that a range of plausible analyses might be made of a given data set for a variety of different purposes. The issue at hand is that of the credibility of an analysis. As we have indicated, the most important consideration in this regard is the extent to which the analysis of the longitudinal data set is both systematic and thorough.

Design and research

Although our emphasis in the above paragraphs has been on ways of justifying the results of design experiments, we do not want to lose sight of the fact that design research is about researching and designing. We have discussed issues such as validity and trustworthiness at some length and much of the current debate about design research has focused on justification.[5] However, the design aspect of the methodology is equally important. Design research presupposes that there is an adequately grounded basis for designing the innovative learning ecology/instructional sequence. The description "learning ecology," introduced by Cobb *et al.* (2003), might be more adequate as it emphasizes that we are dealing with a complex, interacting system involving multiple elements of different types and levels – by designing these elements and anticipating how these elements function together to support learning. Taking into account the complexity of a learning ecology, this implies the need for a very broad framework. The research of Doerr and Zangor (2000) serves to illustrate the complexity of a learning ecology. The authors found that productive use of graphic calculators requires coherence between the following elements of a learning ecology:

- the beliefs of the teacher
- the ability of the teacher to work with the graphic calculator
- the classroom culture (social norms and sociomath norms), and social practices
- the design of the instructional sequence
- the characteristics of the instructional tasks
- the manner in which the graphic calculator is construed as a tool
- the pedagogical–didactic skills of the teacher in making this whole system work.

In light of this list, it can be argued that the theoretical base for the design should incorporate general background theories such as socioconstructivism, or sociocultural theory, domain-specific theory and theories on specific elements of the learning ecology, such as theories on tool use.

In addition to this the research team should be well informed about state-of-the-art professional knowledge of the domain under consideration.

Acknowledgement

The analysis reported in this paper was supported by the National Science Foundation under grant no. REC REC 0231037. The opinions expressed do not necessarily reflect the view of the Foundation.

Notes

1 This corresponds with the types two and three in the discussion paper of Gravemeijer and van den Akker (2003).
2 Similar efforts have been made in science education (Lijnse 1987). Coincidentally, van den Akker and colleagues developed a more general design-theory-oriented form of design research in the Netherlands, which they also called "developmental research" (van den Akker 1999).
3 The prefix *domain-specific* is used to delineate RME from general instructional theories, and to express that this theory is specific to the domain of mathematics education.
4 We initially worked with univariate data. When we moved to bi-variate data we were not able to identify or find any research report that we could build on.
5 This seemed to be the case at the symposium Design-Based Research: Grounding a New Methodology, at the AERA 2004.

References

Atkinson, P., Delamont, S., and Hammersley, M. (1988). Qualitative research traditions: A British response to Jacob. *Review of Educational Research, 58*, 231–50.

Bakker, A. (2004). *Design Research in Statistics Education, on Symbolizing and Computer Tools*. Utrecht: CDß Press.

Ball, D. (1993). With an eye on the mathematical horizon: Dilemmas of teaching elementary school mathematics. *Elementary School Journal, 93*, 373–97.

Brown, A. L. (1992). Design experiments: Theoretical and methodological challenges in creating complex interventions in classroom settings. *The Journal of the Learning Sciences, 2*(2), 141–78.

Bruner, J. (1994). *Four Ways to Make Meaning*. Invited Address at the AERA Conference 1994, New Orleans.

Cobb, P. (1999). Individual and collective mathematical development: The case of statistical data analysis. *Mathematical Thinking and Learning, 1*(1), 5–44.

Cobb, P., Confrey, J., diSessa, A., Lehrer, R., and Schauble, L. (2003). Design experiments in education research. *Educational Researcher, 32*(1), 9–13.

Cobb, P., Gravemeijer, K., Yackel, E., McClain, K., and Whitenack, J. (1997). Symbolizing and mathematizing: The emergence of chains of signification in one first-grade classroom. In D. Kirshner and J. A. Whitson (eds), *Situated Cognition Theory: Social, Semiotic, and Neurological Perspectives* (pp. 151–233). Mahwah, NJ: Lawrence Erlbaum Associates.

Cobb, P. and Hodge, L. L. (2003, April). *An interpretive scheme for analyzing the identities that students develop in mathematics classrooms*. Paper presented at the annual meeting of the American Educational Research Association, Chicago.

Cobb, P., McClain, K., and Gravemeijer, K. P. E. (2003). Learning about statistical covariation. *Cognition and Instruction, 21*(1), 1–78.

Cobb, P. and Steffe, L. P. (1983). The constructivist researcher as teacher and model builder. *Journal for Research in Mathematics Education, 14*(2), 83–95.

Cobb, P., Stephan, M., McClain, K., and Gravemeijer, K. (2001). Participating in classroom mathematical practices. *Journal of the Learning Sciences, 10*(1–2), 113–64.

Cobb, P. and Whitenack, J. (1996). A method for conducting longitudinal analyses of classroom video recordings and transcripts. *Educational Studies in Mathematics, 30*, 213–28.

Cobb, P. and Yackel, E. (1996). Constructivist, emergent, and sociocultural perspectives in the context of developmental research. *Educational Psychologist, 31*, 175–90.

Cobb, P., Yackel, E., and Wood T. (1989). Young children's emotional acts while doing mathematical problem solving. In D. McLeod and V. M. Adams (eds), *Affect and Mathematical Problem Solving: A New Perspective* (pp. 117–48). New York: Springer.

diSessa, A. A. (1992). Images of learning. In E. De Corte, M. C. Linn, H. Mandl, and L. Verschaffel (eds), *Computer-Based Learning Environments and Problem Solving* (pp. 19–40). Berlin: Springer.

diSessa, A. A. (2002). Students' criteria for representational adequacy. In K. Gravemeijer, R. Lehrer, B. van Oers, and L. Verschaffel (eds), *Symbolizing, Modeling and Tool Use in Mathematics Education* (pp. 105–29). Dordrecht: Kluwer Academic Publishers.

diSessa, A. A. and Cobb, P. (2004). Ontological innovation and the role of theory in design experiments. *The Journal of the Learning Sciences, 13*(1), 77–103.

Doerr, H. M. and Zangor, R. (2000) Creating meaning for and with the graphing calculator. *Educational Studies in Mathematics, 41*, 143–63.

Freudenthal, H. (1971). Geometry between the devil and the deep sea. *Educational Studies in Mathematics, 3*, 413–35.

Freudenthal, H. (1973). *Mathematics as an Educational Task*. Dordrecht: Reidel.

Freudenthal, H. (1983). *Didactical Phenomenology of Mathematical Structures*. Dordrecht: Reidel.

Freudenthal, H. (1991). *Revisiting Mathematics Education*. Dordrecht: Kluwer Academic Publishers.

Freudenthal, H., Janssen, G. M., and Sweers, W. J. (1976). *Five Years IOWO on H. Freudenthal's Retirement from the Directorship of IOWO: IOWO Snapshots*. Dordrecht: Reidel.

Glaser, B. G. and Strauss, A. L. (1967). *The Discovery of Grounded Theory: Strategies for Qualitative Research*. New York: Aldine.

Gravemeijer, K. P. E. (1993). The empty number line as an alternative means of representation for addition and subtraction. In: J. de Lange, I. Huntley, C. Keitel, and M. Niss (eds), *Innovation in Mathematics Education by Modeling and Applications* (pp. 141–59). Chichester: Ellis Horwood.

Gravemeijer, K. P. E. (1994). *Developing Realistic Mathematics Education*. Utrecht: Cdß Press.

Gravemeijer, K. (1998). Developmental Research as a Research Method. In J. Kilpatrick and A. Sierpinska (eds), *What is Research in Mathematics Education and What are its Results? ICMI Study Publication; Book 2* (pp. 277–95). Dordrecht: Kluwer Academic Publishers.

Gravemeijer, K. (1999). How emergent models may foster the constitution of formal mathematics. *Mathematical Thinking and Learning, 1*(2), 155–77.

Gravemeijer, K. and van den Akker, J. (2003, December). *How to review proposals for design research?* Working document for the PROO workshop, Amsterdam.

Hiebert and Stigler (1999). *The Teaching Gap*. New York: Free Press.

Kessels, J. P. A. M. and Korthagen, F. A. J. (1996). The relation between theory and practice: Back to the classics. *Educational Researcher, 25*, 17–22.

Lijnse, P. L. (1987). Onderzoek, ontwikkeling en ontwikkelingsonderzoek: In en na het PLON. *Panama-Post. Tijdschrift voor Nascholing en Onderzoek van het Reken-Wiskundeonderwijs, 6*(1), pp. 35–43.

Maxwell, J. A. (2004). Causal explanation, qualitative research, and scientific inquiry in education. *Educational Researcher, 33*(2), 3–11.

Meira, L. (1995). The microevolution of mathematical representations in children's activity. *Cognition and Instruction, 13*, 269–313.

Moore, D. S. (1997). New pedagogy and new content: The case of statistics. *International Statistical Review, 65*(2), 123–65.

NCTM Research Advisory Committee (1996). Justification and reform. *Journal for Research in Mathematics Education, 27*(5), 516–20 (Emotional acts?).

Sfard, A. (1991). On the dual nature of mathematical conceptions: Reflections on processes and objects as different sides of the same coin. *Educational Studies in Mathematics, 22,* 1–36.

Shadish, W. R., Cook, T. D., and Campbell, D. T. (2002). *Experimental and Quasi-*

Experimental Designs for Generalized Causal Inference. Boston: Houghton Mifflin.

Simon, M. A. (1995). Reconstructing mathematics pedagogy from a constructivist perspective. *Journal for Research in Mathematics Education, 26*, 114–45.

Smaling, A. (1990). Enige aspecten van kwalitatief onderzoek en het klinisch interview (Some aspects of qualitative research and the clinical interview). *Tijdschrift voor Nascholing en Onderzoek van het Reken-Wiskundeonderwijs, 8*(3), 4–10.

Smaling, A. (1992). Varieties of methodological intersubjectivity – the relations with qualitative and quantitative research, and with objectivity. *Quality & Quantity, 26*, 169–80.

Steffe, L. P. (1983). The teaching experiment methodology in a constructivist research program. In: M. Zweng, T. Green, J. Kilpatrick, H. Pollak, and M. Suydam (eds), *Proceedings of the Fourth International Congress on Mathematical Education* (pp. 469–71). Boston: Birkhäuser.

Stephan, M., Bowers, J., Cobb, P., and Gravemeijer, K. (eds) (2003). *Supporting students' development of measuring conceptions: Analyzing students' learning in social context. Journal for Research in Mathematics Education*, Monograph No. 12. Reston, VA: National Council of Teachers of Mathematics.

Streefland, L. (1990). *Fractions in Realistic Mathematics Education, a Paradigm of Developmental Research*. Dordrecht: Kluwer Academic Publishers.

Taylor, S. J. and Bogdan, R. (1984). *Introduction to Qualitative Research Methods: The Search for Meanings* (second edition). New York: Wiley.

Thompson, A. G. and Thompson, P. W. (1996). Talking about rates conceptually, part II: Mathematical knowledge for teaching. *Journal for Research in Mathematics Education, 27*, 2–24.

Thompson, P. W. and Thompson, A. G. (1994). Talking about rates conceptually, part I: A teacher's struggle. *Journal for Research in Mathematics Education, 25*, 279–303.

Treffers, A. (1987). *Three Dimensions: A Model of Goal and Theory Description in Mathematics Instruction – The Wiskobas Project*. Dordrecht: Reidel.

Tzou, C. (2000). *Learning about data creation*. Paper presented at the annual meeting of the American Educational Research Association, New Orleans.

van den Akker, J. (1999). Principles and methods of development research. In J. van Akker, R. M. Branch, K. Gustafson, N. Nieveen, and T. Plomp (eds), *Design Approaches and Tools in Education and Training* (pp. 1–14). Boston: Kluwer Academic Publishers.

Yackel, E. and Cobb, P. (1996). Sociomathematical norms, argumentation, and autonomy in mathematics. *Journal for Research in Mathematics Education, 27*, 458–77.

Chapter 4

Design research from a technology perspective

Thomas C. Reeves

The effectiveness of the field known as educational technology in fundamentally enhancing teaching and learning has increasingly been called into question, as has the efficacy of educational research in general. Doubts about educational technology research primarily stem from decades of an arguably flawed research agenda that has been both pseudoscientific and socially irresponsible. It is proposed that progress in improving teaching and learning through technology may be accomplished using *design research* as an alternative model of inquiry. Design research protocols require intensive and long-term collaboration involving researchers and practitioners. It integrates the development of solutions to practical problems in learning environments with the identification of reusable design principles. Examples of design research endeavors in educational technology are described here. The chapter ends with a call for the educational technology research community to adopt design research methods more widely.

Introduction

Educational technology as a field of study and area of practice emerged in the wake of World War II, although its roots are sometimes traced as far back as the 1920s (Saettler 1990). (For the purposes of this chapter, educational technology and instructional technology are considered synonymous, although subtle distinctions exist in the literature (Reiser and Ely 1997).) Originally built on the foundations of the behaviorist theories of Watson, Skinner, Hull, and others, the earliest innovations created by educational technologists and their collaborators, such as educational films, programmed instruction, and instructional television, were viewed by their creators and early adopters as having enormous potential to improve education. As the foundations of the underlying learning theories changed from behaviorism to cognitive learning theory and eventually social constructivism, and new technologies such as computer-assisted instruction and web-based learning environments emerged, ever more optimistic promises were made about the capacity of educational technology to improve education across all levels in diverse contexts. However, thousands of individual research studies and large-scale meta-analyses of these studies (Bernard *et al.* 2004; Dillon and Gabbard 1998; Fabos and Young 1999) have clearly demonstrated that educational technology has not even begun to reach its widely promoted potential, and, in recent years, skepticism about the effectiveness of this field has steadily increased (Cuban 2001; Noble 2001; Oppenheimer 2003).

The perceived failure of educational technology cannot be isolated from the assessment in some quarters that educational research and development as a whole has been a failed enterprise, at least in the United States of America. The U.S. Department of Education under the federal administration of President George W. Bush has shown its disdain for past educational research and development by agreeing with the politically conservative Coalition for Evidence-Based Policy (2002: 1) that "over the past 30 years the United States has made almost no progress in raising the achievement of elementary and secondary school students ... despite a 90 percent increase in real public spending per student." But such attacks do not arise solely from those who are politically motivated. The cover story of the 6 August 1999 edition of *The Chronicle of Higher Education*, the weekly newspaper of record for North American academics, decried "The failure of educational research" (Miller 1999). The article claimed that educational researchers waste the vast resources spent on their research, employ weak research methods, report findings in inaccessible language, and issue statements that are more often contradictory than not.

Indeed, the educational research community has often been its own worst enemy as a result of focusing more on establishing the legitimacy of one educational research tradition over another (such as the long-term struggle among the adherents of quantitative, qualitative, and critical methodological paradigms) rather than on improving education *per se*. As just one example of this infighting, Lagemann (2000) argued that, in a misguided effort to be recognized as being truly "scientific," educational researchers have turned away from the pragmatic vision of John Dewey, whereas Egan (2002) contended that the progressive ideas of Dewey and others are largely responsible for the general ineffectiveness of schools in North America.

Contentiousness within the educational research and development community is most obvious today with respect to arguments about the value and feasibility of randomized controlled trials (RCTs), used in medical research, as an approach capable of guiding progress in education. Slavin (2002), among others, asserted that the remarkable progress evident in the last 100 years of medical practice could be achieved in education if only educational researchers would adopt that same randomized experimental trials approach to revealing "what works." Slavin (2002: 19) optimistically proclaimed "Once we have dozens or hundreds of randomized or carefully matched experiments going on each year on all aspects of educational practice, we will begin to make steady, irreversible progress." Slavin failed to sufficiently acknowledge the frequent failures of medical research. For example, Ioannidis (2005) found that one-third of the most frequently cited clinical research studies published in three prestigious medical journals (*JAMA*, *New England Journal*, and *Lancet*) between 1990 and 2003 reported positive findings that were contradicted by later research or found to have exaggerated effects.

In response to Slavin (2002) and other proponents of RCTs in education (for example, National Research Council (2002)), Olson (2004) argued that double-blind experiments, although feasible in medicine, are impossible in education. He further questioned the viability of RCTs in educational contexts on the basis that implementation variance reduces treatment differences, causal agents are underspecified, and the goals, beliefs, and intentions of students and teachers affect treatments to a much greater extent than the beliefs of patients affect pharmaceuticals and other medical treatments. Chatterji (2004) maintained that the emphasis on RCTs and the establishment of a "What Works Clearinghouse" "ignore the critical realities about social, organizational, and policy environments in which educational programs and interventions reside." She advocated "decision-oriented" evaluation research over "conclusion-oriented" academic research, and recommended extended-term mixed-method (ETMM) designs as a viable alternative.

Despite these and other criticisms, the U.S. Department of Education and federal agencies such as the National Science Foundation have apparently assumed the primacy of RCTs, as evidenced by the fact that their most recent funding requirements mandate the use of the "scientific" methods advocated by Slavin (2002) and others. The American Evaluation Association is just one of several professional organizations that have taken issue with this direction at the U.S. federal level, concluding that the priority given to randomized trials:

> manifests fundamental misunderstandings about (1) the types of studies capable of determining causality, (2) the methods capable of achieving scientific rigor, and (3) the types of studies that support policy and program decisions. We would like to help avoid the political, ethical, and financial disaster that could well attend implementation of the proposed priority.
>
> (American Evaluation Association 2003)

Perhaps Slavin (2002), Feuer *et al.* (2002), and others who promote the expenditure of millions of dollars on RCTs in education should consider the conclusions drawn about educational research by the renowned philosopher of science, Thomas Kuhn, who said:

I'm not sure that there can now be such a thing as really productive educational research. It is not clear that one yet has the conceptual research categories, research tools, and properly selected problems that will lead to increased understanding of the educational process. There is a general assumption that if you've got a big problem, the way to solve it is by the application of science. All you have to do is call on the right people and put enough money in and in a matter of a few years, you will have it. But it doesn't work that way, and it never will.

(quoted in Glass and Moore (1989: 1))

If the proponents of RCTs discount Kuhn, perhaps they will find the later work of Lee Cronbach, one of the most eminent educational researchers of the last half of the twentieth century, more credible (Cronbach 1982; Cronbach *et al.* 1980). After decades of experimental research, Cronbach came to the conclusion that we could not pile up generalizations from numerous small-scale studies fast enough to meaningfully apply the results in specific classrooms at a specific time. Simply put, Cronbach (1975: 125) cautioned that "when we give proper weight to local conditions, any generalization is a working hypothesis, not a conclusion."

In light of the conclusions of experts such as Kuhn and Cronbach, it is frustrating to see renewed enthusiasm for RCTs and other forms of experimental research in education. Educational researchers appear to be unable to learn from their past history of inconsequential impact on practice. As Labaree lamented:

One last problem that the form of educational knowledge poses for those who seek to produce it is that it often leaves them feeling as though they are perpetually struggling to move ahead, but getting nowhere. If Sisyphus were a scholar, his field would be education. At the end of long and distinguished careers, senior educational researchers are likely to find that they are still working on the same questions that confronted them at the beginning. And the new generation of researchers they have trained will be taking up these questions as well, reconstructing the very foundation of the field over which their mentors labored during their entire careers.

(Labaree 1998: 9)

The state of educational technology research

Given the difficulty of conducting any sort of educational research (Berliner 2002), it should not surprise anyone that educational technology research has yielded as dismal a record as other areas of educational inquiry. The reality of educational technology research is that isolated researchers primarily conduct *one-off* quasi-experimental studies rarely linked to a robust research agenda, much less concerned with any relationship to practice.

These studies, often focused on alternative media treatments (for example, online versus face-to-face instruction) or difficult-to-measure individual differences (for example, self-regulated learning), are initially presented as papers at conferences attended by educational technology researchers, and eventually published in academic journals that few people read. As in many other contexts for educational inquiry, educational technology research has been plagued by a history of *no significant differences*, and even the most thorough meta-analyses of the quasi-experimental research studies conducted by educational technologists yield effect sizes that are extremely modest at best (Bernard *et al.* 2004; Dillon and Gabbard 1998; Fabos and Young 1999).

Reeves (1995) reviewed 5 years of research papers published in two of the premier educational research journals of that time (*Educational Technology Research and Development* and the *Journal of Computer-Based Instruction*), and found that the majority of the published studies had predictive goals of testing hypotheses derived from theory or comparing one medium for instructional delivery with another. Despite the fact that these journals were refereed, Reeves found that most of the studies used flawed quasi-experimental designs and/or weak quantitative measures of the primary variables related to achievement, attitudes, or other outcomes. One result of the generally pseudoscientific nature of much of the published literature in educational technology is that when other researchers conduct meta-analyses of these studies, they often find that they must reject upwards of 75 percent of the published literature for a variety of failings (Bernard *et al.* 2004; Dillon and Gabbard 1998; Fabos and Young 1999). Among the weaknesses in the ubiquitous media comparison studies are specification error, lack of linkage to theoretical foundations, inadequate literature reviews, poor treatment implementation, major measurement flaws, inconsequential learning outcomes for research participants, inadequate sample sizes, inaccurate statistical analyses, and meaningless discussions of results (Reeves 1993).

Bernard *et al.* (2004) conducted a comprehensive meta-analysis of empirical comparisons of distance education courses with face-to-face instruction courses between 1985 and 2002. Although they found more than 1,000 comparison studies in the research literature, the majority of the studies did not meet their criteria for inclusion in the meta-analysis. Using the reduced set of papers focused on measures of student achievement, Bernard *et al.* detected a very small, but statistically significant, positive mean effect size for interactive distance education compared to traditional classroom instruction. Further analysis indicated that synchronous communication and two-way audio and video were among the conditions that contributed to effective interactive distance education. While this meta-analysis is one of the best of its kind, its findings, as well as those derived from other related meta-analyses (Cavanaugh 2001; Machtmes and Asher 2000), fall far short with respect to specifying design guidelines for practitioners.

The kind of media comparison research synthesized in most meta-analyses has a long and dubious history in educational technology (Clark 1983, 2001). Saettler (1990) found evidence of experimental comparisons of educational films with classroom instruction as far back as the 1920s, and comparative research designs have been applied to every new educational technology since then. As evidenced by the 1,000 plus quasi-experimental studies of distance education versus traditional methods examined by Bernard *et al.* (2004), this ultimately futile approach to educational research is well entrenched in the minds and work habits of educational technology researchers. Indeed, despite frequent admonitions against it, media comparison studies continue to be published in one guise or another (Koory 2003; MacDonald and Bartlett 2000; Scheetz and Gunter 2004; Summers *et al.* 2005). *No significant differences in learning* has been the most consistent result. Educational technology researchers would do well to heed Sir John Daniel who wrote:

> the futile tradition of comparing test performances of students using new learning technologies with those who study in more conventional ways … is a pointless endeavor because any teaching and learning system, old or new, is a complex reality. Comparing the impact of changes to small parts of the system is unlikely to reveal much effect and indeed, "no significant difference" is the usual result of such research.
>
> (Daniel 2002: x)

In the face of this legacy of ill-conceived and poorly conducted research that results in no significant differences or, at best, modest effect sizes, even journalists can build a strong case against the endeavors of educational technologists and others to promote the use of technology in education. For example, Todd Oppenheimer wrote:

> Our [American] desperation for objective information [is] illustrated nowhere more gorgeously than in the field of education. I am speaking of our tendency to promote any new concept by invoking volumes of quantitative "research" that ostensibly proves its value … technology advocates have played it expertly when it comes to claims about what computers will do for student achievement. As it turns out, the vast bulk of their research is surprisingly questionable.
>
> (Oppenheimer 2003: xix)

New research directions for educational technologists

Clearly, there is an urgent need for a better approach to educational technology research. Instead of more media comparison studies, educational technologists should undertake the type of design research that others have labeled "design-based research" (Kelly 2003), "development research" (van den Akker 1999), "design experiments" (Brown 1992; Collins 1992), or "formative research" (Newman 1990). The critical characteristics of "design experiments," as described by Brown (1992) and Collins (1992) are:

- addressing complex problems in real contexts in collaboration with practitioners;
- integrating known and hypothetical design principles with technological advances to render plausible solutions to these complex problems; and
- conducting rigorous and reflective inquiry to test and refine innovative learning environments as well as to define new design principles.

There are major differences between the philosophical framework and goals of both predictive and interpretive traditional educational technology research methods, and design-based research approaches. Van den Akker clarified the differences as follows:

> More than most other research approaches, development research aims at making both practical and scientific contributions. In the search for innovative "solutions" for educational problems, interaction with practitioners ... is essential. The ultimate aim is not to test whether theory, when applied to practice, is a good predictor of events. The interrelation between theory and practice is more complex and dynamic: is it possible to create a practical and effective intervention for an existing problem or intended change in the real world? The innovative challenge is usually quite substantial, otherwise the research would not be initiated at all. Interaction with practitioners is needed to gradually clarify both the problem at stake and the characteristics of its potential solution. An iterative process of "successive approximation" or "evolutionary prototyping" of the "ideal" intervention is desirable. Direct application of theory is not sufficient to solve those complicated problems.
>
> (van den Akker 1999: 8–9).

Reeves (2000) described van den Akker's (1999) conception of design/ development research as a viable strategy for socially responsible research in educational technology. As illustrated in Figure 4.1, even if the results of business-as-usual predictive research in this field provided unassailable results demonstrating the efficacy of educational technology, translating those findings into instructional reform would not be a given. Educational research is usually published in refereed journals that are unread by the vast majority of practitioners. Reading research papers and translating the findings into practical solutions is a formidable task for educational

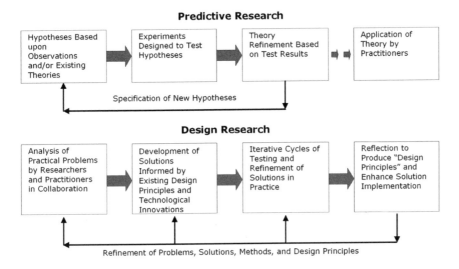

Figure 4.1   Predictive and design research approaches in educational technology
research

practitioners. Also, educational technologists cannot simply install purportedly innovative technologies into the classroom and expect them to work.

One of the primary advantages of design research is that it requires practitioners and researchers to collaborate in the identification of real teaching
and learning problems, the creation of prototype solutions based on existing
design principles, and the testing and refinement of both the prototype solutions and the design principles until satisfactory outcomes have been reached
by all concerned. Design research is not an activity that an individual
researcher can conduct in isolation from practice; its very nature ensures that
progress will be made with respect to, at the very least, clarification of the
problems facing teachers and learners, and ideally, the creation and adoption
of solutions in tandem with the elucidation of robust design models and
principles.

Design research exemplars

Fortunately, a few good examples of design-based research in educational
technology are emerging. The January/February 2005 issue of *Educational
Technology* highlights six of the best-known design-based research initiatives in North America. Squire (2005) presented design-based investigations
of game-based learning environments in which he and his colleagues
employed a blend of quantitative and qualitative methods to explore the
messiness of innovation in authentic contexts. Barab *et al.* (2005) described

how they have applied design-based research methods within the context of the Quest Atlantis project, a noteworthy initiative that not only has produced a rich online learning environment that supports important learning, but has also yielded a promising theoretical framework called Learning Engagement Theory. Nelson *et al.* (2005) clarified the benefits of design-based research with respect to working closely with practitioners in their River City science education project, a curricular level innovation in the form of Multi-User Virtual Environment Experiential Simulators (MUVEES). In describing their Virtual Solar System project, Hay *et al.* (2005) delineated the challenges of design research conducted in a higher education academic environment, including the need to integrate technological innovations with traditional educational artifacts such as textbooks. Hoadley (2005), one of the founders of the Design-Based Research Collective (2003), illustrated how design-based research takes considerable time and patience as his theory of "socially relevant representations" related to learning through discussion has been gradually refined over a decade of inquiry.

A compelling design-based research demonstration of the benefits of collaborating with practitioners to develop innovative educational technologies in the same context in which they will be used is summarized in Kafai's (2005) article titled "The classroom as living laboratory." For decades, educational technologists have developed instructional innovations in laboratories and later inserted them into classrooms with an appalling lack of impact (Cuban 2001). Design-based researchers, by contrast, make a fundamental commitment to developing interactive learning environments in the contexts in which they will be implemented via close collaboration with teachers and students.

The development research of Jan Herrington conducted at Edith Cowan University in Australia (Herrington 1997; Herrington and Oliver 1999) is a rare exemplar of design-based research done by a doctoral student. Herrington employed a range of innovative investigative strategies, including video analysis of the dialogue between pairs of students engaged in multimedia learning. First, she worked with teacher educators to develop a model of the critical factors of situated learning, and then, she instantiated these factors in an innovative multimedia learning environment. Subsequently, she and her collaborators tested the model and the technological products in multiple contexts, including preservice teacher education courses and K–12 schools. This line of research had value within the immediate context of its implementation, and it has also yielded design principles that can be generalized and applied in many other contexts. (Barab and Squire (2004: 6) illustrated how design research of this kind requires both "demonstrable changes at the local level" as well as contributions to theory.) Herrington's research agenda still thrives, recently focusing on the design of authentic activities in web-based learning environments (Herrington *et al.* 2004).

Other notable design-based research dissertations have been undertaken at the University of Twente in the Netherlands. De Vries (2004) conducted four design experiments in primary schools to address the research question: "How can reflection be embedded in the learning process to improve the development of personal understanding of a domain and learning task?" Several years earlier, McKenney (2001) employed development research methods in a large-scale dissertation that addressed the research question: "What are the characteristics of a valid and practical support tool that has the potential to impact the performance of (resource) teachers in the creation of exemplary lesson materials for secondary level science and mathematics education in southern Africa?" Even earlier, Nieveen (1997) pursued development research with the aim of creating a computer support system to assist curriculum developers in optimizing the effectiveness of formative curriculum evaluation efforts. Van den Akker (1999) played important roles in all three of these dissertation studies. These exemplars are especially useful because they clearly demonstrate that, with proper support, doctoral students can engage in fruitful design research within the field of educational technology.

Conditions for reform of educational technology research

For design research to be taken seriously by the educational technology research community, fundamental changes in our methods of research and development are recommended. The kinds of design/development research described by van den Akker (1999), Bannan-Ritland (2003), Barab and Squire (2004), and others hold great promise. But other changes are needed. For example, the conceptualization of learning theory as something that stands apart from and above instructional practice should be replaced by one that recognizes that learning theory can be collaboratively shaped by researchers and practitioners in context. This shift in our way of thinking about research and theory as processes that can be *use-inspired* is taking place in other fields of inquiry as well (Stokes 1997).

In addition, educational technologists may need to rethink their conceptualization of the field as a science (Shavelson *et al.* 2003). Educational technology is first and foremost a design field, and thus design knowledge is the primary type of knowledge sought in this field. Design knowledge is not something that educational researchers derive from experiments for subsequent application by teachers. Design knowledge is contextual, social, and active (Perkins 1986). As a design field, the paramount research goal of education technology should be solving teaching, learning, and performance problems, and deriving design principles that can inform future development and implementation decisions. Our goal should not be to develop esoteric theoretical knowledge that we think practitioners should apply whenever we get around to describing it in practitioner-oriented publications for which researchers usually receive little credit, at least within the traditional academic tenure and promotion review systems. This has not worked for more than 50 years, and it will not work in the future.

Accordingly, the reward structure for scholarship must change in higher education. Educational researchers should be rewarded for participation in long-term development research projects and their impact on practice, rather than for the number of refereed journal articles they publish. In a design field such as educational technology, it is time that we put the *public* back in publication. Academic researchers and the teachers with whom they collaborate must be provided time for participation in design research, reflection, and continuous professional development. Hersh and Merrow (2005) illustrated how the overemphasis on personal research agendas in all fields of academe has led to the decline of teaching and service in higher education in the United States of America over the past 30 years.

Of course, additional financial support is needed for the types of long-term design research initiatives called for in this paper. In the United States of America, the National Science Foundation (www.nsf.gov) and the Institute of Educational Sciences at the Department of Education (www.ed.gov/about/offices/list/ies/index.html) currently maintain that randomized controlled trials are the preferred method for educational research. Hopefully, the kinds of examples presented in this book will encourage authorities at those agencies and other funding sources to consider design research as a viable alternative approach to enhancing the integration of technology into teaching and learning and ultimately improving education for all.

A call for action

Inspired by the design-based research initiatives outlined above and guided by methodologists such as van den Akker (1999), it is time for educational technologists to adopt a more socially responsible approach to inquiry. The design knowledge required in our field is not something that can be derived from the kinds of simplistic, often *one-off*, quasi-experiments that have characterized our shameful legacy of pseudoscience. Without better research, teachers, administrators, instructional designers, policymakers, and others will continue to struggle to use educational technology to reform teaching and learning at all levels.

Who can doubt that the traditional research practices of educational technologists will never provide a sufficient basis for guiding practice? The current situation approaches the absurd. Writing in *Presentations*, a trade magazine aimed at the education and training community, Simons (2004) summarized the multimedia research of Professor Richard Mayer, one of the top researchers working in this area. With insufficient irony, Simons pointed out that Mayer's research (Clark and Mayer 2003; Mayer 2001) supports the use of multimedia in education and training, but also fails to support it! *It depends* seems to be the best response educational technologists pursuing traditional research agendas can provide practitioners. This is not sufficient. There is an important difference between *it depends* and the type of warranted assertions provided by design research. The time to change the direction of educational technology research is now.

References

American Evaluation Association (2003). *American Evaluation Association response to U.S. Department of Education Notice of Proposed Priority, Federal Register RIN 1890-ZA00, Scientifically Based Evaluation Methods.* Document retrieved 29 November 2003 from www.eval.org/doestatement.htm

Bannan-Ritland, B. (2003). The role of design in research: The integrative learning design framework. *Educational Researcher, 32*(1), 21–4.

Barab, S. A., Arici, A., and Jackson, C. (2005). Eat your vegetables and do your homework: A design-based investigation of enjoyment and meaning in learning. *Educational Technology, 65*(1), 15–21.

Barab, S. A. and Squire, K. (2004). Design-based research: Putting a stake in the ground. *The Journal of the Learning Sciences, 13*(1), 1–14.

Berliner, D. C. (2002). Educational research: The hardest science of all. *Educational Researcher, 31*(8), 18–20.

Bernard, R. M., Abrami, P. C., Lou, Y., Borokhovski, E., Wade, A., Wozney, L., Wallet, P. A., Fiset, M., and Huang, B. (2004). How does distance education compare to classroom instruction? A meta-analysis of the empirical literature. *Review of Educational Research, 74*(3), 379–439.

Brown, A. L. (1992). Design experiments: Theoretical and methodological challenges in creating complex interventions in classroom settings. *Journal of the Learning Sciences, 2*, 141–78.

Cavanaugh, C. S. (2001). The effectiveness of interactive distance education technologies in K–12 learning: A meta-analysis. *International Journal of Educational Telecommunications, 7*(1), 73–88.

Chatterji, M. (2004). Evidence on "what works". An argument for extended-term mixed method (ETMM) evaluation designs. *Educational Researcher, 33*(9), 3–13.

Clark, R. C. and Mayer, R. E. (2003). *E-Learning and the Science of Instruction.* San Francisco: Jossey-Bass.

Clark, R. E. (1983). Reconsidering research on learning with media. *Review of Educational Research, 53*(4), 445–59.

Clark, R. E. (ed.) (2001). *Learning from Media: Arguments, Analysis, and Evidence.* Greenwich, CT: Information Age Publishing.

Coalition for Evidence-Based Policy (2002, November). *Bringing Evidence-Based Progress to Education: A Recommended Strategy for the U.S. Department of Education.* Washington, DC: Coalition for Evidence-Based Policy Forum. Report retrieved 1 December 2003 from www.excelgov.org/usermedia/images/uploads/PDFs/coalitionFinRpt.pdf

Collins, A. (1992). Towards a design science of education. In E. Scanlon and T. O'Shea (eds), *New Directions in Educational Technology* (pp. 15–22). Berlin: Springer.

Cronbach, L. J. (1975). Beyond the two disciplines of scientific psychology. *American Psychologist, 30*(2), 116–27.

Cronbach, L. J. (1982). *Designing evaluations of educational and social programs.* San Francisco: Jossey-Bass.

Cronbach, L. J., Ambron, S. R., Dornbusch, S. M., Hess, R. D., Phillips, D. C., Walker, D. F., and Weiner, S. S. (1980) *Toward Reform of Program Evaluation.* San Francisco: Jossey-Bass.

Cuban, L. (2001). *Oversold and Underused: Computers in the Classroom.* Cambridge, MA: Harvard University Press.

Daniel, J. (2002). Preface. In C. Vrasidas and G. V. Glass (eds), *Distance Education and Distributed Learning* (pp. ix–x). Greenwich, CT: Information Age Publishing.

Design-Based Research Collective (2003). Design-based research: An emerging paradigm for educational inquiry. *Educational Researcher, 32*(1), 5–8.

de Vries, B. (2004). *Opportunities for reflection: E-mail and the web in the primary classroom.* Doctoral dissertation, University of Twente: Enschede.

Dillon, A. and Gabbard, R. (1998) Hypermedia as an educational technology: A review of the quantitative research literature on learner comprehension, control and style. *Review of Educational Research, 68*(3), 322–49. www.ischool.utexas .edu/~adillon/publications/hypermedia.html

Egan, K. (2002). *Getting it Wrong from the Beginning: Our Progressivist Inheritance from Herbert Spencer, John Dewey, and Jean Piaget.* New Haven, CT: Yale University Press.

Fabos, B. and Young, M. D. (1999). Telecommunications in the classroom: Rhetoric versus reality. *Review of Educational Research, 69*(3), 217–59.

Feuer, M. J., Towne, L., and Shavelson, R. J. (2002). Scientific culture and educational research. *Educational Researcher, 31*(8), 4–14.

Glass, G. V. and Moore, N. (1989, October). *Research and practice: Universities and schools.* Paper presented at the Second Annual Meeting of the Arizona Educational Research Organization. Retrieved 16 July 2005 from http://glass.ed.asu.edu/gene/ papers/aero.html

Hay, K. E., Kim, B., and Roy, T. C. (2005). Design-based research: More than formative assessment? An account of the Virtual Solar System Project. *Educational Technology, 45*(1), 34–41.

Herrington, J. and Oliver, R. (1999). Using situated learning and multimedia to investigate higher-order thinking. *Journal of Interactive Learning Research, 10*(1), 3–24.

Herrington, J., Reeves, T. C., Oliver, R., and Woo, Y. (2004). Designing authentic activities in web-based courses. *Journal of Computing in Higher Education, 16*(1), 3–29.

Herrington, J. A. (1997). *Authentic Learning in Interactive Multimedia Environments.* Doctoral dissertation, Edith Cowan University: Perth.

Hersh, R. H. and Merrow, J. (2005). *Declining by Degrees: Higher Education at Risk.* New York: Palgrave Macmillan.

Hoadley, C. M. (2005). Design-based research methods and theory building: A case study of research with *SpeakEasy. Educational Technology, 45*(1), 42–47.

Ioannidis, J. P. A. (2005). Contradicted and initially stronger effects in highly cited clinical research. *Journal of the American Medical Association* (JAMA), *294*(2), 218–28.

Kafai, Y. B. (2005). The classroom as "living laboratory": Design-based research for understanding, comparing, and evaluating learning science through design. *Educational Technology*, 65(1), 28–34.

Kelly, A. E. (2003). Research as design. *Educational Researcher*, 32(1), 3–4.

Koory, M. A. (2003). Differences in learning outcomes for the online and F2F versions of "An Introduction to Shakespeare". *Journal of Asynchronous Learning Networks*, 7(2), 18–35. Article retrieved 5 January 2004 from www.aln.org/publications/jaln/v7n2/index.asp

Labaree, D. F. (1998). Educational researchers: Living with a lesser form of knowledge. *Educational Researcher*, 27(8), 4–12.

Lagemann, E. C. (2000). *An Elusive Science: The Troubling History of Educational Research*. Chicago: The University of Chicago Press.

MacDonald, M. and Bartlett, J. E. (2000). Comparison of web-based and traditional delivery methods in a business communications unit. *Delta Pi Epsilon Journal*, 42(2), 90–100.

Machtmes, K. and Asher, J. W. (2000). A meta-analysis of the effectiveness of telecourses in distance education. *The American Journal of Distance Education*, 14(1), 27–46.

Mayer, R. E. (2001). *Multimedia Learning*. New York: Cambridge University Press.

McKenney, S. (2001). *Computer-based support for science education materials developers in Africa: Exploring potentials*. Doctoral dissertation, University of Twente: Enschede.

Miller, D. W. (1999, 6 August). The black hole of educational research: Why do academic studies play such a minimal role in efforts to improve the schools? *The Chronicle of Higher Education*. Retrieved 5 October 2002 from http://chronicle.com

National Research Council (2002). *Scientific Research in Education*. Washington, DC: National Academy Press. Retrieved 23 August 2003 from www.nap.edu/

Nelson, B., Ketelhut, D. J., Clarke, J., Bowman, C., and Dede, C. (2005). Design-based research strategies for developing a scientific inquiry curriculum in a multi-user virtual environment. *Educational Technology*, 65(1), 21–8.

Newman, D. (1990). Opportunities for research on the organizational impact of school computers. *Educational Researcher*, 19(3), 8–13.

Nieveen, N. M. (1997). *Computer support for curriculum developers: A study on the potential of computer support in the domain of formative curriculum evaluation*. Doctoral dissertation, University of Twente: Enschede.

Noble, D. F. (2001). *Digital Diploma Mills: The Automation of Higher Education*. New York: Monthly Review Press.

Olson, D. (2004). The triumph of hope over experience in the search for "what works": A response to Slavin. *Educational Researcher*, 33(1), 24–6.

Oppenheimer, T. (2003). *The Flickering Mind: The False Promise of Technology in the Classroom and How Learning can be Saved*. New York: Random House.

Perkins, D. N. (1986). *Knowledge as Design*. Hillsdale, NJ: Lawrence Erlbaum Associates.

Reeves, T. C. (1993). Pseudoscience in computer-based instruction: The case of learner control research. *Journal of Computer-Based Instruction*, 20(2), 39–46.

Reeves, T. C. (1995). Questioning the questions of instructional technology research. In M. R. Simonson and M. Anderson (eds), *Proceedings of the Annual Conference of the Association for Educational Communications and Technology, Research and Theory Division* (pp. 459–70). Anaheim, CA: Association for Educational Communications and Technology.

Reeves, T. C. (2000). Socially responsible educational technology research. *Educational Technology, 40*(6), 19–28.

Reiser, R. A. and Ely, D. P. (1997). The field of educational technology as reflected through its definitions. *Educational Technology Research and Development, 45*(3), 63–72.

Saettler, P. (1990). *The Evolution of American Educational Technology.* Englewood, CO: Libraries Unlimited.

Scheetz, N. A. and Gunter, P. L. (2004). Online versus traditional classroom delivery of a course in manual communication. *Exceptional Children, 71*(1), 109–20.

Shavelson, R. J., Phillips, D. C., Towne, L., and Feuer M. J. (2003). On the science of education design studies. *Educational Researcher, 32*(1), 25–8.

Simons, T. (2004). The multimedia paradox. *Presentations, 18*(9), 24–26, 28–29.

Slavin, R. E. (2002). Evidence-based education policies: Transforming educational practice and research. *Educational Researcher, 31*(7), 15–21.

Squire, K. D. (2005). Resuscitating research in educational technology: Using game-based learning research as a lens for looking at design-based research. *Educational Technology, 45*(1), 8–14.

Stokes, D. E. (1997). *Pasteur's Quadrant: Basic Science and Technological Innovation.* Washington, DC: Brookings Institution Press.

Summers, J. J., Waigandt, A., and Whittaker, T. A. (2005). A comparison of student achievement and satisfaction in an online versus a traditional face-to-face statistics class. *Innovative Higher Education, 29*(3), 233–50.

van den Akker, J. (1999). Principles and methods of development research. In J. van den Akker, N. Nieveen, R. M. Branch, K. L. Gustafson, and T. Plomp (eds), *Design Methodology and Developmental Research in Education and Training* (pp. 1–14). Dordrecht: Kluwer Academic Publishers.

Chapter 5

Design research from a curriculum perspective

Susan McKenney, Nienke Nieveen and Jan van den Akker

Approaching from a slightly broader perspective than most other discussions of design research in this volume, this chapter contributes to understanding design research in the curriculum domain. It begins by clarifying what is meant by 'curriculum' before characterizing design research from this perspective. The discussion of design research in the curriculum domain builds toward a conceptual model of the process. To illustrate various aspects in the model, three design research cases from the curriculum domain are briefly presented. The chapter concludes with discussion of design research dilemmas, and finally, guidelines for mitigating potential threats to design study rigor.

The curriculum domain

As a field of study, "it is tantalizingly difficult" to know what curriculum is (Goodlad 1994: 1266). Although Taba's (1962) definition of a "plan for learning" is generally accepted, dispute abounds with regard to further elaboration of the term (Marsh and Willis 1995). In this chapter, the notion of curriculum is treated from an inclusive perspective. That is, the broad definition of a plan for learning has been used as a starting point, while related views have been sought to enhance the understanding of curriculum. The remainder of this section presents the curricular perspectives that most robustly underpin our vision of design research in the curriculum domain.

Perspectives

How does one go about planning for learning? Curricular decision making is generally an iterative and lengthy process, carried out by a broad range of participants and influenced by an even wider variety of stakeholders. Curricular decisions may be analyzed from various angles; Goodlad (1994) defines three: sociopolitical, technical-professional, and substantive. The sociopolitical perspective refers to the influence exercised by various (individual and organizational) stakeholders. The technical-professional perspective is concerned with methods of the curriculum development process, whereas the substantive perspective refers to the classic curriculum question as to *what should be learned?*

The question of what schools should address has confronted society since the dawn of schooling. Curriculum scholars offer numerous perspectives on how the substance of curriculum is determined. Based on the work of Tyler (1949) and subsequent elaborations by others (Eisner and Vallance 1974; Goodlad 1984, 1994; Kliebard 1986; van den Akker 2003; Walker and Soltis 1986), Klep *et al.* (2004) describe three major orientations for selection and priority setting:

- Learner: Which elements seem of vital importance for learning from the personal and educational needs and interests of the learners themselves?
- Society: Which problems and issues seem relevant for inclusion from the perspective of societal trends and needs?
- Knowledge: What is the academic and cultural heritage that seems essential for learning and future development?

Components

Traditionally, curriculum deliberations have focused on the aims and content of learning. Building on broader definitions (Walker 1990) and typologies (Eash 1991; Klein 1991), van den Akker (2003) presents a visual model that illustrates both the interconnectedness of curriculum components and the vulnerability of the structure that connects them (Figure 5.1). At the hub of the model is the rationale, which connects all the other components: aims and objectives, content, learning activities, teacher role, materials and resources, grouping, location, time, and assessment. The spiderweb metaphor emphasizes that, within one curriculum, component accents may vary over time, but that any dramatic shift in balance will pull the entirety out of alignment. Though it may stretch for a while, prolonged imbalance will cause the system to break. Efforts to reform, (re)design, develop, or implement curricula must therefore devote attention to balance and linkages between these ten components.

Consistency, harmony, and coherence

Curriculum concerns may be addressed at various levels: macro (system/ society/nation/state), meso (school/institution), and micro (classroom/ learner). While the spiderweb metaphor emphasizes the need for internal consistency between components, consistency across levels in a system is also a chief concern. This implies that, for example, efforts toward a particular approach to classroom teaching and learning must be designed while taking

Figure 5.1 Curricular spiderweb (van den Akker 2003)

the overarching school and education system into account, or else they risk inconsistent design and – along with that – hindrances to implementation.

Even at differing levels, the ideas bound together in a curriculum may be manifested through various representations. Goodlad *et al.* (1979) distinguished a range of representations, adapted by van den Akker (1988, 1998, 2003), who offers three broad distinctions: the *intended* curriculum, the *implemented* curriculum, and the *attained* curriculum. The intended curriculum contains both the ideal curriculum (the vision or basic philosophy underlying a curriculum) and the formal/written curriculum (intentions as specified in curriculum documents and/or materials). The implemented curriculum contains both the perceived curriculum (interpretations by users, particularly teachers) and the operational curriculum (as enacted in the classroom). The attained curriculum comprises the experiential curriculum (learning experiences from pupil perspective) and the learned curriculum (resulting learner outcomes).

High-quality curriculum development strives for internal consistency with regard to curricular components (spiderweb elements) and levels (micro through macro), as well as harmony among curricular representations (intended through attained). High-quality curriculum development also reflects system coherence. That is, within the context for which a curriculum

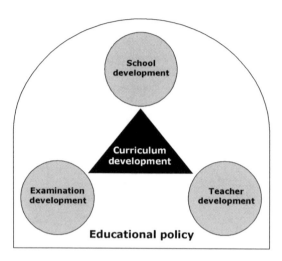

Figure 5.2   System coherence

is intended, curricular decision making is influenced by a thorough understanding of the system elements that most influence curriculum enactment: teacher capacity and (large-scale) pupil assessment (Figure 5.2).

Much research has been conducted to explore how the teacher shapes the curriculum (Clandinin and Connelly 1992; Eisenhart and Borko 1991; Zumwalt 1988); and while conclusions vary, there is little debate that teacher capacity influences the enactment of curriculum. In exploring the fit between a curricular innovation and the system in which it functions, alignment with pre- and in-service teacher education is critical to successful implementation. Additionally, experience and research alike (Black and Atkin 1996) attest to the notion that external examinations wield some of the strongest influences on curriculum implementation. This aspect of system coherence is, with surprising frequency, downplayed – or in more extreme cases – ignored, as further discussed below.

The issue of system coherence often presents a struggle for developers of innovative curricula. For example, an in-depth discovery-learning curriculum designed for use where state examinations tend to favor relatively shallow but extremely broad content knowledge would not be coherent at the system level. But strong beliefs in the benefits of discovery learning might prompt curriculum developers to take on the implementation challenges associated with such inconsistency. In these situations, teacher development tends to be seen as the primary vehicle for compensating for curricular vulnerability. While this may be viable, it does·not represent robust curriculum design. From an implementation perspective, robust curriculum design is evidenced by attention to the three criteria discussed in this section:

- consistency among curricular components (spiderweb) and across levels (macro, meso, and micro);
- harmony between representations (intentions, implementations, and attainments); and
- coherence within the system context (factoring in the influences of teacher development, school development, and large-scale assessment).

Curriculum implementation

Around the globe and particularly in the areas of science and mathematics education, curricula have undergone several waves of renewal in the past few decades. A major reform period began following the launch of Sputnik and continued on until the 1970s (in some cases, even longer); this period was earmarked by innovations taking place on a large scale. However, despite concerted efforts, many improvement projects were considered failures (for a synthesis of curriculum implementation research from this era, see Fullan and Pomfret (1977)). Perhaps in part due to disappointing results in the past, the 1980s saw a shift to debates on accountability and the most appropriate forms of curricular reform. Changing societal concerns as well as new scientific insights fueled these debates. The 1990s bore witness to a rebirth of large-scale reform, tempered by cautions resulting from failed efforts in the past. In this most recent wave of reform, systemic, sustainable change receives the main focus. A core element of this focus is the careful consideration of new (and/or improved) implementation strategies, which have been addressed in literature (Confrey *et al.* 2000; Fullan 2000; van den Akker 1998).

Throughout earlier waves of curriculum reform, most study of curriculum implementation took place from a fidelity perspective. Researchers focused on measuring the degree to which a particular innovation was implemented as planned, and on identifying the factors that facilitated or hindered the implementation (Snyder *et al.* 1992). Implementation research has led to an appreciation for the perspectives of mutual adaptation and – in more recent years – enactment. Mutual adaptation (Berman and McLaughlin 1977, 1978) suggests that curriculum implementation is a process whereby adjustments to a curriculum are made by curriculum developers and those who actually use it in a school or classroom context. Curriculum enactment, on the other hand, views curriculum as the educational experience jointly created by students and teachers. From this perspective, the role of the teacher is that of a curriculum developer who, with time, according to Snyder *et al.* (1992: 418), "grows ever more competent in constructing positive educational experiences." A teacher's ability to construct such experiences is helped or hindered by the quality of the externally created curriculum (which may be highly specified or may contain broad guidelines). Yet, one's own professional capacities yield even stronger influences on this process. The enactment perspective is becoming increasingly widespread (Ball and Cohen 1996; Barab and Leuhmann 2003; Ben-Peretz 1990, 1994; Clandinin and Connelly 1992; Fullan 2000) and forms the cornerstone of our vision on design research in the curriculum domain.

Design research in the curriculum domain

Having described core elements in our understanding of curriculum, design research in this domain is now addressed. This section describes why design research is usually chosen; what outputs result from its undertaking; when this kind of approach is useful; who is generally involved; where it takes place; and how it is conducted. Thereafter, a conceptual model for design research in the curriculum domain is presented.

Why choose a design research approach?

Numerous motives for design research have been cited in this volume and elsewhere. Many of them speak to the long-standing criticism that educational research has a weak link with practice. Increasingly, experts are calling for research to be judged not only on the merits of disciplined quality, but also on the adoption and impact in practice (Design-Based Research Collective 2003; Kelly 2004; Reeves *et al.* 2005). In combination with other approaches, design research has the potential to help develop more effective educational interventions, and to offer opportunities for learning during the research process. In the curriculum domain, design research is often selected to help improve understanding of how to *design for implementation*. By carefully studying successive approximations of ideal interventions in their target settings, insights are sought on how to build and implement consistent, harmonious, and coherent components of a robust curriculum (as described in the previous section, p. 68).

What are the outputs of design research?

In considering what design research in the curriculum domain ought to produce, it may be useful to return to the aforementioned orientations of knowledge, society, and learner. The primary output of design research is the resulting knowledge that is generated; this usually takes the form of design principles. The secondary output of design research in this domain is its societal contribution: curricular products or programs that are of value to schools or a broader education community. The tertiary output, related to the learning orientation, is the contribution made by design research activities themselves to the professional development of participants. Design research thus contributes to three types of outputs: design principles, curricular products (or programs), and professional development of the participants involved, as illustrated in Figure 5.3.

Design principles

The knowledge claim of design research in the curriculum domain takes the form of design principles (Linn *et al.* 2004; van den Akker 1999), also known as domain theories (Chapter 7), heuristics (Design-Based Research Collective 2003), or lessons learned (Vanderbilt, Cognition and Technology Group 1997). While the format may vary, design principles generally offer the kinds of heuristic guidelines described by van den Akker:

> If you want to design intervention X [for purpose/function Y in context Z]; then you are best advised to give that intervention the characteristics C, C, ..., C [substantive emphasis]; and do that via procedures P, P, ..., P [procedural emphasis]; because of theoretical arguments T, T, ..., T; and empirical arguments E, E, ... E.
>
> (van den Akker 1999)

Design principles are not intended as recipes for success, but to help others select and apply the most appropriate substantive and procedural knowledge for specific design and development tasks in their own settings.

Curricular products

To some extent (substantive) knowledge about essential characteristics of an intervention, can be distilled from the secondary output of design research in this domain – curricular products. Design research contributes to designing, developing, and improving the quality of curricular products

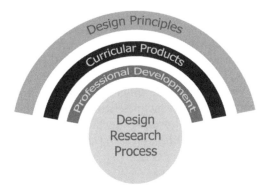

Figure 5.3 Three main outputs of design research

(or programs). For specific recommendations on improving quality, see the "How is design research conducted?" section later in this chapter (p. 76). The range of curricular products is commensurate with the breadth of the domain's scope. Some examples include: manifestations of the written curriculum (for example, national syllabus or teacher guide); materials used in the classroom (for example, instructional booklets or software for pupils); or professional development aids (for example, online environments for teacher communities).

Professional development

When research methods are creatively and carefully designed, they can contribute to the tertiary output of design research – professional development of participants. For example, data collection methods, such as interviews, walk-throughs, discussions, observations, and logbooks, can be structured to stimulate dialogue, reflection or engagement among participants. This perspective also stems from the conviction that there is a natural synergy between curriculum development and teacher development, and that sensitivity to this can provide more fruitful research and development opportunities. Because of the implications for research design, further discussion of this issue is subsequently addressed in the "How is design research conducted?" section (p. 76).

When is this approach useful?

As illustrated in Figure 5.4, design research in the curriculum domain utilizes the outputs of validation studies, which provide the necessary starting points (for example, theories and perspectives) for beginning to engage in design based on scientific insights. Design research is especially warranted when existing knowledge falls short, as is often the case with highly innovative curriculum improvement initiatives. The main aim of design research in these situations is to develop new knowledge that can help construct pioneering curricular solutions that will prove to be viable in practice. Because of the focus on understanding curriculum enactment and the implementation process, this kind of study rarely includes large-scale effectiveness research. However, effectiveness studies are necessary to understand long-term impact and provide valuable information pertaining to the quality of the outputs (design principles, curricular products, and professional development) of curriculum design research. For further discussion of validation and effectiveness studies, please refer to Chapter 10.

Who is involved in design research?

Though hardly universal, many studies in curriculum design and implementation create space for (varying degrees of) participatory design. In particip-

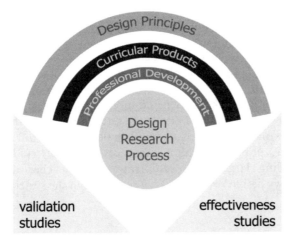

Figure 5.4   Design research on curriculum, flanked by validation and effectiveness studies

atory design, the end users of curriculum contribute to the design process. This means that researcher insights are augmented by those offered by such participants as pupils, teachers, school leaders, and external experts. Until recently, the bulk of these contributions tended to come during the generation of initial design specifications (analysis) and refinement of draft products (formative evaluation). While the movement to directly involve teachers in the design process has been gaining momentum since the 1970s (Stenhouse 1980), it would seem that only in the last decade have researchers begun to seriously consider how to marry the interests of teachers in a participatory design process and reap the relevance benefits without putting the methodological quality of the research in jeopardy (McKenney 2001; McKenney and van den Akker 2005; van den Akker 2005).

Where does design research take place?

Researchers have found that practices or programs developed in one setting can often be used successfully in other places (Loucks-Horsley and Roody 1990). But despite the potential insights to be gained through exploration of how ideas may be translated for use in other settings, it should be noted that such a task is far from easy. "There is no (and never will be any) silver bullet" for educational change in varying contexts (Fullan 1998). Neglecting to seriously understand and consider the "fit" of an innovation is a common cause for failure (Guthrie 1986).

Contextual understanding is essential for robust curriculum design.

Because the real-world settings of schools and classrooms tend to be so complex and unpredictable, the only way to sincerely explore curricular products is by involving stakeholders (see "Who is involved in design research?", p. 74) in the target context (Design-Based Research Collective 2003; McKenney 2001; Richey and Klein 2005; van den Akker 1999). Based on careful analysis, design principles offer situated guidelines, which rely on accurate, thorough portrayal of pertinent contextual variables. Design research must therefore take place in naturally occurring test beds to address usability issues and intimately portray the setting for which the design was created. Contextual variables that should be portrayed include local factors (school climate, pupil population, resources available, etc.) and system factors (including large-scale examinations and teacher development). Figure 5.5 shows design research taking place within the system for which it is intended.

How is design research conducted?

Tackling design research is no easy task. But, as in responsible curriculum development, it can be useful to begin by articulating the underlying philosophy before addressing the process itself. This section therefore begins by describing the tenets that form the foundation of the design research approach described here, and then addresses the iterative nature of the design research process.

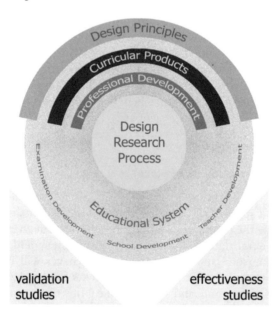

Figure 5.5   Design research taking place in context

Tenets

As previously mentioned, design research efforts contribute to three main types of outputs: design principles, curricular products, and the professional development of participants. Related to each output, we define a set of tenets to shape design research in the curriculum domain (respectively): rigor, relevance, and collaboration.

- Rigor – As noted in Chapter 10, and in the "What are the outputs of design research?" section of this chapter (p. 72), design research yields knowledge in the form of design principles. For these to be valid and reliable, the research from which they are distilled must adhere to rigorous standards. The wealth of literature on naturalistic research (Miles and Huberman 1994; Patton 1990; Yin 1994) offers much support for addressing issues of internal validity (extent to which causal relationships can be based on the findings), external validity (extent to which findings are transferable to some broader domain), reliability (extent to which the operations of the study can be repeated with the same results), and utilization (extent to which action could be taken based on the findings).
- Relevance – The societal contribution of design research refers to the curricular product or program that benefits educational practice. As mentioned earlier in this chapter, curricular products must be carefully examined and, if necessary, (re)tailored for the context and culture in which they will be implemented. When it comes to design research (McKenney 2001; McKenney and van den Akker 2005), such efforts must be based on a working knowledge of the target setting and be informed by research and development activities taking place in naturally occurring test beds.
- Collaboration – If design research activities are to contribute to the professional development of participants, then design and development must be conducted in *collaboration with* and not *for* those involved. Additionally, data collection procedures should be mutually beneficial – addressing research needs while simultaneously offering meaningful experiences for the participants. As mentioned previously, data collection methods such as interviews, walk-throughs, discussions, observations, and logbooks can be structured to stimulate dialogue, reflection, or engagement among participants.

Iterations

There is little debate that, in any domain, the design research process tends to be iterative (Cobb *et al.* 2003; Design-Based Research Collective 2003; Reeves *et al.* 2005; van den Akker 1999). In the curriculum domain, each iteration helps sharpen aims, deepen contextual insights, and contribute to the three main outputs (design principles drafted, curricular products improved, and opportunities for professional development created). Within each iteration, the classic cycle of analysis, design, and evaluation takes place as illustrated in Figure 5.6.

ANALYSIS ⇒ GAP CLOSURE

Analysis in the curriculum domain is conducted to understand how to target a design. It primarily features assessment of harmony (or discord) between the aforementioned intended, implemented, and attained curricula. Further study of internal consistency (macro, meso, and micro level) and system coherence (alignment with teacher development and pupil assessment) often sheds light on how and where gaps between representations are created. Additionally, good analysis makes use of inputs such as creativity, inspiring examples, and a systematic approach. In design *research*, good analysis includes these features, but is also more forcefully driven by theoretical and empirical insights (often, but not exclusively, from validation studies as mentioned previously). Once completed, the analysis findings usually offer guidelines for design that target the closure of one or more gaps between the intended, implemented, and attained curricula. These guidelines take the form of design specifications that will shape curricular products such as

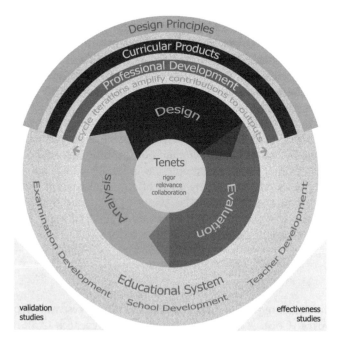

Figure 5.6 Analysis, design, and evaluation cycle shaped by tenets at the core

standards descriptions, textbooks, and learner toolkits. In some cases, the guidelines also shape the development process.

DESIGN ⇒ PROTOTYPE STAGES

The iterative nature of design research is due, in part, to the dominance of a prototyping approach. Prototyping has traditionally been associated with engineering and is a well-proven method for solving real problems. Over time, this approach has spread to other arenas that apply a systematic approach to problem solving and design, including education. Ranging from "formative experiments" (Newman 1990; Reinking and Watkins 1996), to iterative revision (McKenney 2001; Nieveen 1997; Nieveen and van den Akker 1999), prototyping refers to when design products are evaluated and revised through a systematic process.

Various forms of prototypes based on differing stages of development have been identified in literature (Connel and Shafer 1989; Nieveen 1999). In earlier iterations, the product of the design stage may be an initial prototype that globally demonstrates the nature of the design. As development continues, prototypes may be partially or even completely elaborated. At the conclusion of a design cycle, a product's stage of development (global, partial, or complete prototype) influences the kind of formative evaluation activities that may take place.

EVALUATION ⇒ TRADE-OFFS

Formative evaluation is performed to improve (instead of prove) the quality of prototypes. Depending on the stage of development (global, partial, or complete), evaluation approaches may include: developer screening, expert review, micro evaluation, and/or classroom tryouts. Participants in evaluation activities can include the educational designers themselves, other members of the development team (graphic designers, software engineers, etc.), experts, teachers, pupils, parents, and any other relevant stakeholder group.

While specific criteria for exploring (ways to improve) the quality of a prototype vary along with the aims of the curricular product, the following three general criteria, rooted in earlier work (Blumenfeld *et al.* 2000; Fishman and Krajcik 2003; Fishman *et al.* 2004; McKenney 2001; McKenney and van den Akker 2005; Nieveen 1997; Nieveen and van den Akker 1999), can be useful: viability, legitimacy, and efficacy. These are summarized in Figure 5.7.

Viability relates predominantly to the implementability of a design. While viability can best be tested through the (formative) evaluation of draft products, consideration of viability aspects is a recommended starting point for drafting and refining design intentions. Three aspects of viability are distinguished: practicality, relevance, and sustainability. Viability questions include: Will this design be realistically usable in everyday *practice*? Is this

Criteria	Aspects
Viability	Practicality
	Relevance
	Sustainability
Legitimacy	Contemporary scientific insights
	Consistency, harmony & coherence
Efficacy	Yields desired results
	Cost benefit ratio

Figure 5.7   Generic quality criteria for evaluation of curricular designs

design *relevant* to the needs and wishes of those in the target setting? May one expect this design (or its use) to be *sustainable*? The criterion of legitimacy relates to the underlying intentions; legitimacy aspects are investigated through questions such as: Is (the rationale behind) this design based on *contemporary scientific insights*? Are the design components *internally consistent*? Does the design support *coherence* among system factors? Efficacy relates to how well a design yields the desired result(s). Because efficacy is defined in terms of the aims of a design, the criteria for efficacy vary by case. For example, if a curricular product is intended to foster the development of classroom management skills, then impact on classroom management skills would be one of the criteria to look for in evaluation. Some generic efficacy questions include: Is the time, effort, and financial *cost* worth the investment? How (in)efficient is (the use of) this design?

Insights gleaned from evaluation activities focused on the viability, legitimacy, and efficacy provide inputs for subsequent redesign of curricular prototypes. More often than not, a renewed analysis must take place as trade-off decisions are made. For example, a design may prove to be highly legitimate and effective, but not viable (for example, too expensive or too time-consuming) in practice. If viability can be achieved, but only with costs to legitimacy or efficacy, then trade-offs must be weighed. Without a balance among these three, implementation will be challenged or possibly fail.

Conceptual model

The model for design research in the curriculum domain (Figure 5.8) is based on the previous discussion. At the heart of the process are the tenets of research rigor, local relevance, and collaboration with participants. These foundational ideas shape the analysis, design, and evaluation cycle. Triangular flows indicate principle outputs from one phase that influence the subsequent phase, specifically: contextual analysis leads to design targets for closing gaps between the intended, implemented, and attained curricula; prototype stage of development has implications for framing an evaluation;

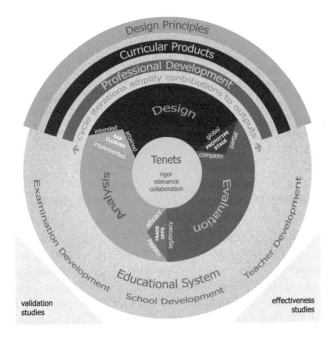

Figure 5.8 Conceptual model of design research in the curriculum domain

and evaluation insights help to deliberate over trade-off decisions between the viability, legitimacy, and efficacy quality aspects. Design research cycle iterations contribute to the aforementioned outputs of professional development, curricular products, and design principles. While this all takes place within and is influenced by the target context, design principles that are well articulated (and carefully portray the context) may be useful in other settings. Finally, this kind of research relies on the results of validation studies to provide relevant scientific insights to help shape the design (legitimacy); this type of research further provides starting points for larger-scale effectiveness studies to explore long-range impact.

Examples

This model (Figure 5.8) has its roots in the topics discussed throughout the first two sections of this chapter. Numerous studies have also been based on these and related ideas. Although articulated and visualized in this format for the first time here, the conceptual model shown in Figure 5.8 aptly depicts the research approach used in several curriculum studies; three of these are briefly described below.

For comparison purposes, the examples selected share main elements of an

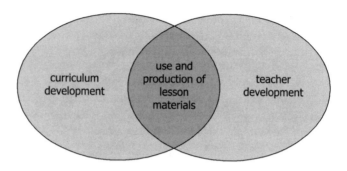

Figure 5.9 Conceptual framework shared by the three example studies

underlying rationale. As shown in Figure 5.9, the three studies all explore support for curriculum development and teacher development at a naturally occurring crossroads: the use and production of lesson materials.

Each of the studies yielded design principles, curricular products, and contributed to the professional development of participants. They were all conducted in the target context, using a synthesis of literature and previous research as major points of departure. Cycles of analysis, design, and evaluation took place in all three cases, and these were shaped by the need for research rigor, contextual relevance, and collaboration with the participants. While they all aimed to contribute to (improved) development of curriculum materials and teacher professional development, their iterative cycle activities were conducted differently and each resulted in different types of curricular products; these are briefly described in Table 5.1.

Please visit www.routledge.com to access this book's supplemental website, containing information on the research design and approach used in each of these three studies.

Table 5.1 Examples of design research in the curriculum domain

	Iterations	*Curricular product*
Cascade-Sea	Two analysis cycles, four design cycles and two evaluation cycles	Software tool to help (facilitator) teachers create teacher guides
Tomc@t	Three full cycles of analysis, design and evaluation	ICT-based learner materials to foster early literacy
Mac	Two smaller and three larger cycles of (re)design and evaluation	Teacher guides for secondary level science

Design research dilemmas

In the curriculum domain, a design research approach is often chosen because of the opportunities it offers to help improve educational realities directly (through the curricular products designed and the professional development opportunities created by the study itself) and indirectly (through design principles to inform future endeavors). While the overall benefits of this approach are perceived to be worth the investments, design studies are subject to challenges not typically encountered through more conventional approaches. This section addresses three: designer as implementer and evaluator; real-world research brings real-world complications; and the warrants and risks associated with adaptable study design.

Designer (also) as implementer and evaluator

Due to the nature of the approach (prototyping in context), design researchers often find themselves playing the conflicting roles of advocate and critic (Design-Based Research Collective 2003). The multiple roles can be extremely useful, for example, during formative evaluation. When designers participate in the formative evaluation activities, they are afforded the opportunity to gain deeper and often sharper insights into the strengths and weaknesses of a design. This has the potential to shorten both the lines of communication within a development team and the time needed for revision decisions. However, the methodological concerns would seem obvious. Despite efforts to stimulate criticism, the fact that the designer and evaluator may be the same person increases the chance for an evaluator effect (Patton 1990). Participants may react differently due to the designer's presence during formative evaluation; and the designers may be (unintentionally) less receptive to critique. Regardless of efforts made to obtain neutrality, value-free research will not be possible when the designer performs evaluation activities. "Rather than pretending to be objective observers, we must be careful to consider our role in influencing and shaping the phenomena we study. This issue is obvious when individuals take on multiple roles of researchers; teachers; teachers of teachers" (Putnam and Borko 2000: 13). Acknowledging the inevitable impact of researchers (especially those donning multiple, even conflicting roles) on the context in which understanding is sought is a first step toward combating associated obstacles, such as (Krathwohl 1993): the Hawthorne effect (involvement in the study makes participants feel special and thereby influences their behavior); hypothesis guessing (participants try to guess what the researcher seeks and react accordingly); and diffusion (knowledge of the treatment influences other participants). Thereafter, these threats may be further reduced by striving for unobtrusiveness through making the research setting as natural and as genuine as possible.

Real-world research settings bring real-world complications

As stated previously, design research makes use of naturally occurring test beds. The benefits of conducting research in authentic settings would seem obvious: the more realistic the research setting, the more the data will reflect reality. But deeper understandings come at the (potential) cost of losing control over data collection rigor. For example, if pilot teachers share their enthusiasm with colleagues, who in turn request to join the participant group, researchers are faced with a dilemma: compromise the sample or encourage teamwork? When researcher interests are no longer the only ones at stake, compromise is imminent.

Particularly when a "cultural stranger" (Choksi and Dyer (1997) in Thijs (1999)) attempts to carry out research in a foreign setting, the degree to which an *outsider* can conduct meaningful research must be addressed. In many situations, participants are sometimes hesitant to be completely open with researchers from different cultural contexts. Toward earning participant trust and building an understanding of the context, the importance of collaboration and mutually beneficial activities cannot be overemphasized, as these are the two main avenues available to a researcher who prioritizes the *insider* perspective. This is not to say that being an outsider is completely without advantages. In some situations, it actually allows for a degree of objectivity and, along with that, a freedom (or forgiveness) for honesty that is not permitted to those within a particular group.

Adaptability

Design research is often mapped by evolutionary planning. Given the aforementioned real-world research settings, adaptability is essential. Furthermore, it is important that research cycles be responsive to findings from previous ones. Yet, a research design that keeps changing is weak. The notion of evolutionary planning refers to a sound planning framework that is responsive to field data and experiences at acceptable moments during the course of a study. The need for adaptability in design research pertains not only to planning, but also to the role of the researcher during the study. According to van den Akker (2005), the synergy between research and practice can be maximized when researchers demonstrate adaptability by: (i) being prepared, where desirable, to take on the additional role of designer, advisor, and facilitator, without losing sight of their primary role as researcher; (ii) being tolerant with regard to the often unavoidably blurred role distinctions and remaining open to adjustments in the research design if project progress so dictates; and (iii) allowing the study to be influenced, in part, by the needs and wishes of the partners, during what is usually a long-term collaborative relationship. Such adaptability requires strong organizational and communicative capacities on behalf of the researcher.

Adaptability also requires sound understanding of research rigor so that prudent changes and choices that maximize value and minimize threats to quality are made.

Design study guidelines

Earlier in this chapter, three tenets that lay the foundation for design research initiatives were discussed: rigor, relevance, and collaboration. Related to the previous section on design research dilemmas (p. 83), this chapter concludes by addressing some guidelines for guarding academic rigor while still conducting relevant, collaborative inquiry. These guidelines may help generate credible, trustworthy, and plausible design principles.

Explicit conceptual framework

As with all sound research, design research activities should be rooted in an underlying rationale. The underlying rationale should evolve through formal activities (for example, literature review and interviewing experts) as well as informal activities (discussions with critical friends and during conferences). This should lead to an explicit conceptual framework, providing the conceptual framework gives others the opportunity to make analytic generalizations (external validity).

Congruent study design

In a congruent study design, the chain of reasoning (Krathwohl 1993) is both transparent and tight. This means that the structure of the study as a whole demonstrates clear and strong links between previous research, theory, research questions, research design, data analysis, and conclusions. In studies with a congruent design, the ideas supporting each of these components are compatible.

Triangulation

During each iteration of a design study, various individuals may participate and an assortment of data collection methods must be carefully chosen and applied; these are applications of triangulation. According to several authors (Merriam 1988; Miles and Huberman 1994; Patton 1990) triangulation assists in enhancing the reliability and internal validity of the findings. This effect rests on the premise that the weaknesses in each single data source, method, evaluator, theory, or data type will be compensated by the counterbalancing strength of another. This is one strategy that can help speak specifically to concerns associated with the multiple, sometimes blurred roles taken on by design researchers. Triangulation of data sources, data collection settings, instruments, or even researchers can be quite robust, but should not be driven by the misconception that more is better. This notion is aptly conveyed by Dede (2004: 107) who notes, "everything that moved within a 15-foot radius of the phenomenon was repeatedly interviewed, videotaped, surveyed and so-forth – and this elephantine effort resulted in the birth of mouse-like insights in their contribution to educational knowledge."

Inductive and deductive data analysis

As with other forms of research, it can be useful to tackle data analysis from differing perspectives. Often, both deductive and inductive analyses are useful. Deductive analyses classify data according to existing schemes, usually based on the conceptual framework, and inductive analyses explore emergent patterns in the data. Interim analysis (following a phase or cycle) is essential for informing subsequent efforts. Repeated interim analysis is referred to as "sequential analysis" by Miles and Huberman who comment as follows on the strengths and weaknesses of this approach:

> Their [interim analyses'] strength is their exploratory, summarizing, sense-making character. Their potential weaknesses are superficiality, premature closure, and faulty data. These weaknesses may be avoided through intelligent critique from skeptical colleagues, feeding back into subsequent waves of data collection.
>
> (Miles and Huberman 1994: 84)

Data analysis may further be bolstered when conducted or revisited by a team of researchers or critical friends. Finally, insights stemming from only one participant may be extremely useful, even if not echoed by others. While frequency of findings is a good indicator of importance, data analysis procedures must be sensitive to the salience and depth of findings.

Full description

Another tactic mentioned by several authors (Merriam 1988; Miles and Huberman 1994) is providing a context-rich description of the situation, design decisions, and research results. While the generalizability of design research findings is limited, full descriptions will help the readers of such portraits gain insight on what happened during research stages and make inferences based on (or transfer) the findings to other situations (external validity). In addition, a full description may also make replications possible. If the replication of a study led to similar results, this would demonstrate that the study was reliable.

Member check

Merriam (1988) states that taking data and interpretations back to the source may increase the internal validity of the findings. For instance, participants of a tryout can be invited to provide feedback on an outline with the major results of the tryout. Likewise, it can be useful when interviewees review a researcher's synopsis of an interview, and provide corrections if necessary.

Concluding comments

This chapter set out to contribute to understanding of design research in the curriculum domain. Essential to understanding the ideas presented here on design research are the perspectives discussed at the start of the chapter pertaining to the nature of curriculum, how it is built, and what factors affect its implementation. This lens demonstrates that curriculum design and design research in this domain cannot be decoupled from the system in which these activities take place. This calls for both design and research work to be conducted *in situ*, together with the participants (teachers, pupils, etc.). The yields – design principles, curricular products and professional development of participants – can make the effort worthwhile, but care must be taken to guard the rigor of a research process that is subjected to the complexities of the real world. Some tactics for coping with these challenges were offered in the last section of this chapter, but these represent only an initial set of guidelines based on existing approaches to research. Further work is needed to better understand this emerging field and to provide additional guidelines as well as examples. In the meantime, it is hoped that this chapter and the related website examples will further dialogue on design research from the curriculum perspective.

References

Ball, D. and Cohen, D. (1996). Reform by the book: What is – or might be – the role of curriculum materials in teacher learning and instructional reform? *Educational Researcher*, 25(9), 6–8, 14.

Barab, S. and Leuhmann, A. (2003). Building sustainable science curriculum: Acknowledging and accommodating local adaptation. *Science Education*, 87(4), 454–67.

Ben-Peretz, M. (1990). *The Teacher-Curriculum Encounter*. Albany: State University of New York Press.

Ben-Peretz, M. (1994). Teachers as curriculum makers. In T. Husén and T. Postlethwaite (eds), *The International Encyclopedia of Education* (pp. 6089–92). Oxford: Pergamon.

Berman, P. and McLaughlin, M. (1977). *Federal Programs Supporting Educational Change. Volume vii. Factors Affecting Implementation and Continuation*. Santa Monica: Rand Corporation.

Berman, P. and McLaughlin, M. (1978). *Federal Programs Supporting Educational Change. Volume viii. Implementing and Sustaining Innovations*. Santa Monica: Rand Corporation.

Black, P. and Atkin, J. (eds) (1996). *Changing the Subject: Innovations in Science, Mathematics and Technology Education*. London: Routledge.

Blumenfeld, P., Fishman, B. J., Krajcik, J., Marx, R. W., and Soloway, E. (2000). Creating usable innovations in systemic reform: Scaling up technology-embedded project-based science in urban schools. *Educational Psychologist, 35*(3), 149–64.

Choski, A. and Dyer, C. (1997). North-south collaboration in educational research: Reflections on an Indian experience. In M. Crossley and G. Vuillamy (eds), *Qualitative Research in Developing Countries* (pp. 265–93). New York: Garland Publishing.

Clandinin, J. and Connelly, M. (1992). Teacher as curriculum maker. In P. Jackson (ed.), *Handbook of Research on Curriculum* (pp. 363–401). New York: Macmillan.

Cobb, P., Confrey, J., diSessa, A., Lehrer, R., and Schauble, L. (2003). Design experiments in educational research. *Educational Researcher, 32*(1), 9–13.

Confrey, J., Castro-Filho, J., and Wilhelm, J. (2000). Implementation research as a means to link systemic reform and applied psychology in mathematics education. *Educational Psychologist, 35*(3), 179–91.

Connel, J. and Shafer, L. (1989). *Structured Rapid Prototyping: An Evolutionary Approach to Software Development*. Englewood Cliffs, NJ: Yourdan Press.

Dede, C. (2004). If design-based research is the answer, what is the question? *Journal of the Learning Sciences, 13*(1), 105–14.

Design-Based Research Collective (2003). Design-based research: An emerging paradigm for educational inquiry. *Educational Researcher, 32*(1), 5–8.

Eash, M. (1991). Curriculum components. In A. Lewy (ed.), *The International Encyclopedia of Curriculum* (pp. 71–3). Oxford: Pergamon.

Eisenhart, M. and Borko, H. (1991). In search of an interdisciplinary collaborative design for studying teacher education. *Teaching and Teacher Education, 7*(2), 137–57.

Eisner, E. and Vallance, E. (1974). *Conflicting Conceptions of Curriculum*. Berkeley: McCutchan.

Fishman, B. and Krajcik, J. (2003). What does it mean to create sustainable science curriculum innovations? A commentary. *Science Education, 87*(4), 564–73.

Fishman, B., Marx, R. W., Blumenfeld, P., Krajcik, J., and Soloway, E. (2004). Creating a framework for research on systemic technology innovations. *Journal of the Learning Sciences, 13*(1), 43–76.

Fullan, M. (1998). The meaning of educational change: A quarter of a century of learning. In A. Hargreaves, A. Lieberman, M. Fullan, and D. Hopkins (eds), *International Handbook of Educational Change* (pp. 214–28). Dordrecht: Kluwer Academic Publishers.

Fullan, M. (2000). The return of large-scale reform. *Journal of Educational Change, 1*, 1–23.

Fullan, M. and Pomfret, A. (1977). Research on curriculum and instruction implementation. *Review of Educational Research, 47*(2), 335–97.

Goodlad, J. (1984). *A Place Called School*. Highstown, NJ: McGraw-Hill.

Goodlad, J. (1994). Curriculum as a field of study. In T. Husén and T. Postlethwaite (eds), *The International Encyclopedia of Education* (pp. 1262–7). Oxford: Pergamon.

Goodlad, J., Klein, M., and Tye, K. (1979). The domains of curriculum and their study. In J. Goodlad *et al.* (eds), *Curriculum Inquiry: The Study of Curriculum Practice* (pp. 43–76). New York: McGraw-Hill.

Guthrie, G. (1986). Current research in developing countries: The impact of curriculum reform on teaching. *Teaching and Teacher Education*, 2, 81–9.

Kelly, A. (2004). Design research in education: Yes, but is it methodological? *Journal of the Learning Sciences*, *13*(1), 115–28.

Klein, F. (1991). A conceptual framework for curriculum decision making. In F. Klein (ed.), *The Politics of Curriculum Decision Making: Issues in Centralizing the Curriculum* (pp. 24–41). Albany: State University of New York Press.

Klep, J., Letschert, A., and Thijs, A. (2004). *Wat Gaan We Leren? [What Will We Learn?]*. Enschede: Stichting Leerplanontwikkeling (SLO).

Kliebard, H. (1986). *The Struggle for the American Curriculum, 1893–1958*. Boston: Routledge & Kegan Paul.

Krathwohl, D. (1993). *Methods of Educational and Social Science Research: An Integrated Approach*. New York: Longman.

Linn, M., Davis, E., and Bell, P. (2004). *Internet Environments for Science Education*. London: Lawrence Erlbaum Associates.

Loucks-Horsley, S. and Roody, D. (1990). Using what is known about change to inform the regular education initiative. *Remedial and Special Education*, *11*(3), 51–6.

Marsh, C. and Willis, G. (1995). *Curriculum: Alternative Approaches, Ongoing Issues*. Englewood Cliffs, NJ: Merrill.

McKenney, S. (2001). *Computer based support for science education materials developers in Africa: Exploring potentials*. Doctoral dissertation, University of Twente: Enschede.

McKenney, S. and van den Akker, J. (2005). Computer-based support for curriculum designers: A case of developmental research. *Educational Technology Research and Development*, *53*(2), 41–66.

Merriam, S. (1988). *Case Study Research in Education*. San Francisco: Jossey-Bass.

Miles, M. and Huberman, M. (1994). *Qualitative Data Analysis*. London: Sage.

Newman, D. (1990). Opportunities for research on the organizational impact of school computers. *Educational Researcher*, *19*(3), 8–13.

Nieveen, N. (1997). *Computer-based support for curriculum developers: A study on the potential of computer support in the domain of formative curriculum evaluation*. Doctoral dissertation, University of Twente: Enschede.

Nieveen, N. (1999). Prototyping to reach product quality. In J. van den Akker, R. Branch, K. Gustafson, N. Nieveen, and T. Plomp (eds), *Design Approaches and Tools in Education and Training* (pp. 125–36). Dordrecht: Kluwer Academic Publishers.

Nieveen, N. and van den Akker, J. (1999). Exploring the potential of a computer tool for instructional developers. *Educational Technology Research and Development*, *47*(3), 77–98.

Patton, M. (1990). *Qualitative Evaluation and Research Methods*. Newbury Park, CA: Sage.

Putnam, R. and Borko, H. (2000). What do new views of knowledge and thinking have to say about research on teacher learning? *Educational Researcher, 29*(1), 4–15.

Reeves, T., Herrington, J., and Oliver, R. (2005). Design research: A socially responsible approach to instructional technology research in higher education. *Journal of Computing in Higher Education*, 16(2), 97–116.

Reinking, D. and Watkins, J. (1996). *A formative experiment investigating the use of multimedia book reviews to increase elementary students' independent reading. Reading research report no. 55 (also available as Eric document # 398 570)*. Athens, GA: National Reading Research Center, College of Education, The University of Georgia.

Richey, R. and Klein, J. (2005). Developmental research methods: Creating knowledge from instructional design and development practice. *Journal of Computing in Higher Education*, 16(2), 23–38.

Snyder, J., Bolin, F., and Zumwalt, K. (1992). Curriculum implementation. In P. Jackson (ed.), *Handbook of Research on Curriculum* (pp. 402–35). New York: Macmillan.

Stenhouse, L. (ed.) (1980). *Curriculum Research and Development in Action*. London: Heinemann.

Taba, H. (1962). *Curriculum Development: Theory and Practice*. New York: Harcourt, Brace & World.

Thijs, A. (1999). *Supporting science curriculum reform in Botswana: The potential of peer coaching*. Doctoral dissertation, University of Twente: Enschede.

Tyler, R. (1949). *Basic Principles of Curriculum and Instruction*. Chicago: University of Chicago Press.

van den Akker, J. (1988). *Ontwerp en Implementatie van Natuuronderwijs [Design and Implementation of Science Education]*. Lisse: Swets & Zeitlinger.

van den Akker, J. (1998). The science curriculum: Between ideals and outcomes. In B. Fraser and K. Tobin (eds), *International Handbook of Science Education* (pp. 421–47). Dordrecht: Kluwer Academic Publishers.

van den Akker, J. (1999). Principles and methods of development research. In J. van den Akker, R. Branch, K. Gustafson, N. Nieveen, and T. Plomp (eds), *Design Approaches and Tools in Education and Training* (pp. 1–14). Dordrecht: Kluwer Academic Publishers.

van den Akker, J. (2003). Curriculum perspectives: An introduction. In J. van den Akker, W. Kuiper, and U. Hameyer (eds), *Curriculum Landscapes and Trends* (pp. 1–10). Dordrecht: Kluwer Academic Publishers.

van den Akker, J. (2005). Hoe kan samenwerking leiden tot meer succes en wijsheid in onderwijsontwikkeling? [How can collaboration lead to more success and wisdom in education development?]. *Pedagogische Studiën*, 82(4), 343–7.

Vanderbilt, Cognition and Technology Group (1997). *The Jasper Project: Lessons in Curriculum, Instruction, Assessment and Professional Development*. Mahwah, NJ: Lawrence Erlbaum Associates.

Walker, D. (1990). *Fundamentals of Curriculum*. San Diego: Harcourt, Brace Jovanovich.

Walker, D. and Soltis, J. (1986). *Curriculum and Aims*. New York: Teachers College Press.

Yin, R. (1994). *Case Study Research: Design and Methods* (second edition). Beverly Hills, CA: Sage.

Zumwalt, K. (1988). Are we improving or undermining teaching? In L. Tanner (ed.), *Critical Issues in Curriculum: Eighty-Seventh Yearbook of the National Society for the Study of Education* (pp. 148–74). Chicago: University of Chicago Press.

Part 3

Quality

Chapter 6

Assessing the quality of design research proposals
Some philosophical perspectives

D. C. Phillips

Design research (DR), or design experiments, has become the topic of much discussion among educational researchers since the essays by Collins (1992) and Brown (1992). The claim that design of effective and innovative programs or treatments can proceed at the same time as, and is fully integrated with, the pursuit of traditional research objectives, has proved to be somewhat controversial (cf. *Educational Researcher*, 32(1), 2003; *Educational Psychologist*, 39(4), 2004); this is because the simultaneous variation of numerous factors that seems to occur frequently in many of the former endeavors runs counter to the fundamental principle of research, which is to "control the variables." Nevertheless, it clearly seems fruitful for both the production of effective programs and the opening up of interesting (and useful) lines of research to have researchers closely involved in the design process. I am pursuing some of the difficult issues associated with this topic elsewhere (Phillips and Dolle in press), so here I wish to make some preliminary remarks about a related but somewhat neglected matter.

Funding agencies around the world are receiving proposals to carry out design research, and these, of course, need to be evaluated. Assessing the worth of a finalized program, or of a completed research report, is difficult enough, but the problems pale when compared with the difficulties inherent in assessing the quality of *a proposal to carry out* DR. What follows is a brief discussion of some of these, together with some small suggestions that might be helpful.

Education research, and more specifically DR, does not constitute what philosophers call a "natural kind"; it does not form a species with one or a small number of species-defining characteristics. It is a category made by humans for human intellectual, political, and self-identification purposes, and like a hard disk or a file labeled *miscellaneous* it has a lot of different things crammed into it. There are many different types of education research, all of them with their own merits and limitations; and the same can be said of design experiments, which vary enormously in how they manage the relationship between research and development (if this distinction is recognized at all). I do not regard it as productive to spend much time trying to come up with a simple account that ends all controversy about *what design experiments really are* – there is no right answer. For there *is no one thing that they are like.*

To make this clear to potential funders of DR, it may be helpful to refer to the philosopher Wittgenstein's (1963) notion of "family resemblances," one that he illustrated with the concept of "games". (In summary: in defining "games," there is a large set of "family characteristics"; each game instantiates some of the set, but two games might still be games yet have none of these family characteristics in common.) My suggestion is that there will also be a set or family of criteria by which DR should be judged – elements from the set that are appropriate for evaluating one study will not be relevant to another. This does not make the task of the evaluator of research or DR proposals easier, *but it is better to be realistic rather than simplistic.*

There is a well-known issue in assessing research in education relating to the fact that there are many different frameworks or methodological approaches (or, to use the Kuhnian term in its now established, very loose sense, paradigms) within which specific examples of research are located. Thus, the criteria for assessing specific examples often (if not always) need to be framework or paradigm specific, for – to cite an obvious example – the factors that make a piece of ethnography rigorous are not the same factors that mark a good experimental or quasi-experimental study. To make matters more complicated, adherents of one framework or methodological approach often have very little tolerance for rival approaches, so they make unfair judges of such work. Those individuals who fund research, including DR, must somehow overcome any instinctive prejudice they feel about frameworks other than their own favored ones, and, at the very least, they must make a serious effort to appreciate the rationales that are given to justify different styles of work. (There is a limit to tolerance, of course; personally, I have little tolerance for postmodern approaches that often – perhaps not always – reject the entire scientifically oriented research approach and especially the *modernist* notion of reason that underpins it. But the situation is difficult, and the assessor of DR needs to have the wisdom of Solomon!)

There is a serious oversimplification of scientifically oriented research (that probably amounts to an egregious misunderstanding of the nature of scientific inquiry – see Phillips (2005)) that can cloud the assessment of research proposals, including proposals to do DR. (This oversimplification has reached epidemic proportions in the United States of America, where there are very determined efforts to make use of the so-called "gold standard methodology" – namely, the use of randomized controlled experiments or field trials, and as a backup quasi-experiments and regression discontinuity designs – into a necessary condition for funding of research and evaluation by governmental agencies. For examples of favored studies, see the U.S. federally funded "What Works Clearinghouse" at www.W-W-C.org.)

The mistake of oversimplification lies in placing almost all the emphasis on the final stage of a research cycle (the stage of testing or validating the claim that an intervention, treatment or program is causally responsible for some outcome); this is to neglect or even denigrate what the philosopher Reichenbach (1938) many years ago called the "context of discovery", which is the context in which researchers display creativity and do much preliminary investigation (often guided, of course, by deep factual and theoretical background knowledge) in the vital effort to come up with an intervention or treatment that is worth testing.

To put this issue in a slightly different way: the great American pragmatist philosopher, John Dewey, and the critical rationalist philosopher, Karl Popper, gave independent accounts of the logical processes involved in science that are remarkably similar (and, Reichenbach, a logical positivist, would have endorsed their accounts). They saw science as proceeding through cycles, each of which involves identification, clarification and analysis of a problem, analysis of possible solutions, followed by testing the solution or hypothesis that seems most likely to be efficacious (for further discussion and references, see Phillips (1992: chapter 6)). To focus almost entirely upon testing (as in using randomized field trials as *the* gold standard to judge the scientific merit of education research) is to ignore or treat as scientifically insignificant the absolutely crucial earlier stages.

One of the very great virtues of the DR community is that its members take the whole of the scientific research cycle seriously. It will be fatal to the future of DR, and indeed to the future of the whole of science, if funding decisions are to be based entirely, or even just very largely, on the use of a particular family of methods for *testing* hypotheses.

This raises another difficult issue. It is easy to be seduced by a proposal for funding support that focuses upon testing some hypothesis or treatment, for such a proposal will be concrete – it will be quite specific about what will be done. Any competent researcher who focuses on the testing of hypotheses (and not upon their derivation and analysis) will find it easy to specify how the sample will be drawn and from which population it will be drawn, how attrition will be monitored, how the treatment under test will be delivered, and how randomization will be carried out. Such matters can be assessed quite straightforwardly by a potential funding agency. It is much more difficult to assess a proposal that takes the whole scientific cycle seriously, starting with the identification and clarification of a significant problem and moving, via a series of studies and analyses, to a refined hypothesis or treatment that is worthy of being taken seriously enough to be tested.

There are several important subsidiary issues here:

1   Why is this difficult? Simply because it is literally impossible for a person proposing to do an original piece of research to specify in precise terms beforehand what will be done during the early stages of the investigative cycle. Scientific investigation writ large (as opposed to the narrower

domain of hypothesis testing) is not a matter of following a precise algorithm, and the investigator cannot predict at the outset what issues will arise and what opportunities will present themselves. Investigation is a creative, but also necessarily a disciplined, process. Einstein is reported to have remarked that a good scientist is an "unscrupulous opportunist," and Nobel Laureate Percy Bridgman said that "the scientist has no other method than doing his damnedest," but it is difficult for all but the most trusting funding agency to rate highly a proposal that states "I will be an opportunist and do my damnedest" – however, in reality, this is what a good investigator *will* do in the early phases of his or her work. And this is surely what good practitioners of DR do. But to repeat: the damnedest, the opportunism, must be *disciplined*.

2 If the history of science is any guide, it will turn out that the creative processes during what Popper and Dewey identified as the early stages of the scientific inquiry process, and what Reichenbach called the context of discovery – the analyses, the small-scale studies, observations, testing, and probing that occur, the crafting of arguments, and so forth – will often result in the development of such a convincing case (such a convincing *warrant* will be built up) that large-scale hypothesis testing may not be needed at all.

Almost any example from the work of great scientists of the past can be drawn upon as an illustration of the importance of the early phases of a piece of scientific inquiry. Consider the work of William Harvey, who built up – over time – the case that the heart pumps blood, which is carried around the body by arteries and veins. He could not have specified what he was going to do before he did it; at most, he could have indicated that he was interested in investigating why it was that animals have hearts. As problems and criticisms arose, he devised inventive ways to counter them, using a variety of types of study (today we would say that he used mixed methods). Eventually, the warrant for his claim about the circulation of the blood was undeniable – and it is noteworthy that he did not place reliance upon a sole gold standard methodology. It also is sobering to reflect on the fact that he would not have received support from most funding agencies in existence today, because – at the outset of his work – he would not have been able to be specific about what he was going to do. I believe that most if not all design researchers are in the same situation as William Harvey! (The same points could be made in the context of Darwin's or Pasteur's work. See Phillips (2005) for further discussion and references.)

The above discussion leads to the last difficulty I shall raise in the present remarks: in light of the previous points, what advice can I give a funding agency about the criteria they should look for in assessing DR proposals? I seem to have made a strong case (at least I think I have made a strong case) that design researchers, being good scientists whose focus is healthily much wider than mere hypothesis testing, cannot be precise about what they are going to do at the start of their work. So how can an intelligent decision be made about whether to fund a piece of DR? I have three tentative suggestions to offer here.

1 Although it is, in my view, unreasonable to expect a design researcher to be precise about what it is that he or she will actually do in the course of the work, it is not unreasonable to expect some indication of where it is hoped that the main contribution will lie. Let me return to William Harvey: He could say at the outset of his work that he was generally interested in the heart; but note that he did not have several different interests. Design researchers are sometimes not as clear as Harvey; for there is an ambiguity here that runs through much of the DR literature, and needs to be clarified in any DR proposal (for example, this ambiguity bedevils a number of the contributions to the symposium on DR in the *Educational Researcher*, 32(1), 2003). This is the ambiguity over whether the main purpose of a piece of DR is to contribute to an understanding of the *design process* itself (and what this might mean and why it is potentially important ought to be made clear), *or* whether it is to throw light on some educationally relevant phenomenon associated with the program or intervention that is being designed (for example, the learning of certain topics in mathematics by young girls), *or* whether it is to actually design a technically impressive program, intervention, or artifact, *or* to do two or all three of these things. This will be helpful information for a funding agency, which will need to decide if such a purpose (or purposes) falls within its domain of interest. (And, of course, to indicate a general interest at the outset of the work is not to suppose that the focus cannot change as the work proceeds and interesting, new phenomena arise.)

2 The proposal should make clear that the authors understand that the *warrants* supporting the claim that one or the other of these three aims has been achieved, are different. The warrant supporting the claim to have improved the design process is different from the warrant that some aspect of learning has been illuminated, and both of these are different from (but sometimes related to) the warrant for the claim that a technically impressive artifact has been produced. In practice these different purposes are often so intertwined that their different logical/epistemic warranting requirements become seriously confounded. Furthermore, it should be shown that the DR team (for most often it will be more than one individual working on the project) represents the bodies of research and development skills that can reasonably be expected to be needed for such an enterprise, whatever it is. (A study of learning requires different skills from mathematics curriculum development, and the production of rigorous warrants for knowledge claims might require even other skills.)

3 Funding agencies might adopt the way projects are chosen for funding in

the creative arts as their model. A composer being considered for a commission to produce a new symphony cannot be expected to show what the symphony will be like before she has actually composed it! But the composer's portfolio of work can be examined, and the training the composer has received can be investigated. It will be known that this person is good with symphonies for small orchestras but not so proficient in works for the solo violin. It will be known what style of music the particular individual favors (atonal, jazz-oriented, romantic, triumphal, and so forth) and how this fits with the type of work that the commissioning body has in mind. In the end, those awarding the commission place a bet: given the past record (or training or apprenticeship), it is likely that this composer can produce the desired goods. (The MacArthur Foundation does something along these lines with its so-called "genius awards.") This process is fuzzy, but a surprising degree of inter-rater reliability can be achieved between intelligent judges. And it is perhaps the only way to deal with the complexities of the creative scientific process that is central to the design experiment.

I conclude with an optimistic example that illustrates many of the preceding points; it is drawn from a documentary I saw when pursuing my addiction to late-night television. In the period immediately following the end of World War II, the U.S. military, in conjunction with the agency that was the forerunner of NASA, set out to design a plane that could regularly (and safely) fly faster than sound. Not only was it desired to produce a workable product (the X–1 plane), it was also desired to understand the physics – the aerodynamic principles – of flying at speeds greater than Mach 1. In essence, then, the participants were involved in an early piece of design research. It is noteworthy that they obtained funding because the project was a national defense priority and because the participants were experienced in aircraft design and manufacture; they could not (and they did not) specify in detail what they were going to do before they did it – the changes/improvements they made were decided almost on a daily basis. During each test flight, Chuck Yeager, the brash pilot, pushed the prototype to its limits, and afterwards he and his mechanics tinkered to try to increase the speed. (He represented the interests of the military, which were to produce a fast plane as quickly as possible.) The researchers, however, resisted, for after each modification they wanted to carry out a detailed program of testing before further variables were tinkered with (thus illustrating the classic clash between development and research). The situation was alleviated by the use of *two* planes, one for pushing as hard as possible, the other for slower testing. Maybe there is a moral here for design researchers, and their funders.

References

Brown, A. L. (1992). Design experiments: Theoretical and methodological challenges in creating complex interventions in classroom settings. *Journal of the Learning Sciences*, 2, 141–78.

Collins, A. (1992). Toward a design science of education. In E. Scanlon and T. O'Shea (eds), *New Directions in Educational Technology*. New York: Springer.

Phillips, D. C. (1992). *The Social Scientist's Bestiary*. Oxford: Pergamon.

Phillips, D. C. (2005). Muddying the waters: The many purposes of educational inquiry. In C. Conrad and R. Serlin (eds), *Handbook for Research in Education: Engaging Ideas and Enriching Inquiry*, pp. 7–21. Thousand Oaks, CA: Sage.

Phillips, D. C. and Dolle, J. R. (in press). From Plato to Brown and beyond: theory, practice, and the promise of design experiments. In L. Verschaffel, F. Dochy, M. Boekaerts, and S. Vosniadou (eds), *Instructional Psychology: Past, Present and Future Trends. Sixteen Essays in Honour of Erik De Corte*, pp. 275–90. Oxford: Elsevier.

Reichenbach, H. (1938). *Experience and Prediction*. Chicago: University of Chicago Press.

Wittgenstein, L. (1963). *Philosophical Investigations*. Oxford: Blackwell.

Chapter 7

Balancing innovation and risk

Assessing design research proposals

Daniel C. Edelson

In this essay, I consider the question of how to assess proposed design research. In contrast to other authors in this volume, I will approach the question more from the engineer's perspective than from the scientist's perspective. The engineer's approach assumes that one is doing design and development to begin with and asks the question, *what generalizable lessons can one learn from those processes?* The scientist's approach assumes that one is engaged in scientific inquiry about learning and asks the question, *what can one learn by integrating design into the research process that one could not learn otherwise?*

- Scientist's approach to design research in education: How can research be enhanced by integrating iterative design cycles into it?
- Engineer's approach: How can iterative design cycles be used to generate useful research results?

To address the question of how we should assess proposed design research, we must first consider what we can learn from design research and how.

What can we learn from design?

A few years ago I published a paper in the *Journal of the Learning Sciences* on design research with the title, "What do we learn when we engage in design?" In this paper, I took the engineer's perspective on design research. I approached the question with the assumption that design is a learning process. When a design team creates a design to achieve a goal under a set of constraints, they must develop an understanding of the goals and constraints they are designing for, the resources they have available for constructing a design, and the implications of alternative design decisions. In a typical design process, the understanding that the design team develops remains implicit in the decisions they make and the resulting design. I characterize these design decisions as falling into three categories:

- Decisions about the design process: These are decisions about what steps to follow in constructing a design, who to involve, and what roles they should play.
- Assessments of the design context: These are decisions about the goals, needs, and opportunities that must or should be addressed by a design. This category also includes decisions about the design context that must be addressed, such as the challenges, constraints, and opportunities in the context.
- Decisions about the design itself: These are decisions about the design itself. This category includes decisions about how to combine design elements and balance trade-offs in order to meet goals, needs, and opportunities.

While these do not exist in any explicit form in many designs, I find it useful to characterize these sets of decisions as belonging to these three implicit entities. The decisions about the design process can be characterized as comprising a *design procedure*; assessments of the nature of the design context can be characterized as a *problem analysis*; and decisions about the design itself can be characterized as a *design solution*.

The engineering approach to design research assumes that the designer is engaged in these local learning processes and asks how the lessons learned in order to make decisions about the design procedure, problem analysis, and design solution can be made explicit and public to serve the needs of a larger community.

It is important to recognize that the role that design research can play in the larger research endeavor is not hypothesis testing. The appropriate product for design research is warranted theory. As such, the challenge for design research is to capture and make explicit the implicit decisions associated with a design process, and to transform them into generalizable theories. In Edelson (2002), I describe three kinds of theories that can be developed through design research. Each of these corresponds to a set of decisions that designers make:

DOMAIN THEORIES

A domain theory is the generalization of a portion of a problem analysis. There are two types of domain theories:

- A *context theory* is a theory about a design setting, such as a description of the needs of a certain population of students, the nature of certain subject matter, or of the organization of an educational institution.
- An *outcomes theory* describes the effects of interactions among elements of a design setting and possible design elements. An outcomes theory

explains why a designer might choose certain elements for a design in one context and other elements in another.

DESIGN FRAMEWORKS

A design framework is a generalized design solution. It provides guidelines for achieving a particular set of goals in a particular context. A design framework rests on domain theories regarding contexts and outcomes. Van den Akker (1999) also describes design frameworks, which he calls "substantive design principles," as being a product of design research.

DESIGN METHODOLOGY

A design methodology is a general design procedure that matches the descriptions of design goals and settings to an appropriate set of procedures. Van den Akker (1999) calls a design methodology a set of "procedural design principles."

In addition to these three forms of theories, another important product of design research is the design as a case. While it is speculative to generalize from any individual design, an accumulation of related cases can form the basis for making supported generalizations. Therefore, it is important to recognize the value of an individual case of innovative educational design to a larger design research and theory development agenda.

How can we use design as an opportunity to conduct design research?

I've identified four steps to make an educational design process a useful part of theory development. The first is that it should be *research-driven*. That is, the decisions made in the design process should be informed by a combination of prior research and the design researcher's emerging theories. The fact that decisions are informed by prior research does not mean that they must be consistent with the findings of prior research. In fact, a design process may be driven by the desire to question prior research, but it must do so for clear and coherent reasons. Neither does it mean that research exists to inform all or even most design decisions. However, a design researcher should be informed as to where research does and doesn't exist to shape design decisions. Being aware of research increases the likelihood that a design research program will have impact. The second step toward design research is *systematic documentation*. To support the retrospective analysis that is an essential element of design research, the design process must be thoroughly and systematically documented. The third step is *formative evaluation*. Formative evaluation is essential in design research because it can identify weaknesses in the problem analysis, design solution, or design procedure. Ideally, educational design research is conducted in the form of iterative cycles of design, implementation, and formative evaluation. The fourth step toward design research is *generalization*. To generalize, the design researcher must retrospectively analyze the design-specific lessons to identify appropriate generalizations in the form of domain theories, design frameworks, and design methodologies. Being research-driven, maintaining systematic documentation, and conducting formative evaluation all support the process of generalization.

How should we assess proposals for design research?

I now turn to the criteria one might use in assessing proposals for design research. The first criterion is one that applies to any research proposal: if successful, the proposed work must promise to yield insight into an important need or problem. In the case of design research, this insight would take the form of a new or elaborated theory, in contrast to more traditional research, which would most likely take the form of evidence for or against an existing theory. Other proposal evaluation criteria follow from the processes described in the preceding section for using design as an opportunity to conduct research: the proposed design must be grounded in prior research or sound theory; it must have a plan for systematic documentation; it must incorporate formative feedback into a plan for iterative design and development; and, it must allow for a process of generalization based on the other elements of the plan.

These criteria, however, address the research side of design research. Taking the engineering perspective seriously requires that we also consider the design side of a design research proposal. We have to appreciate that design research is inherently exploratory and speculative. It begins with the basic assumption that existing practices are inadequate or can, at least, be improved. This means that new practices are necessary. The underlying questions behind design research are the same as those that drive innovative design:

- What alternatives are there to current educational practices?
- How can these alternatives be established and sustained?

These questions demand a form of research other than traditional empiricism. We cannot apply traditional research methods to these alternative practices because they do not yet exist to be studied.

Since design research is exploratory, it is inherently risky. In fact, design research may lead to designs that are worse than existing practices because they either lead to unsatisfactory outcomes or they are not feasible to implement. This poses a challenge for the evaluation of proposed research because, on the one hand, we want to encourage risk-taking, and on the other we want to limit risk. In order to improve on current practice, we need to take chances on alternatives. In particular, we want to be open to the possibility of dramatically improved outcomes. However, in a resource-limited world, we want to be cautious with resources and use them wisely.

So, how does one apply these conflicting needs regarding risk to the evaluation of design research proposals? First, it is important to distinguish between innovation and risk. The opportunity offered by design research is the opportunity to foster innovation. While the novelty of innovation carries risk, the criterion that design research should be research-driven helps mitigate that risk. If the proposed design is grounded in existing research or sound theory, then it can be innovative without being overly risky. If it is not well grounded, then, it may, in fact, be too speculative and carry too much risk. On the other hand, if the design concept at the heart of a design research proposal is not sufficiently innovative, then it may not be worth the investment. In short, a design research proposal must involve design that is innovative enough to explore territory that cannot be explored with traditional means, but it must be guided by sound theory, to insure that it is not overly speculative.

A second way to manage risk is through the ongoing evaluation that should be part of design research. Thus, the nature of the evaluation plan must be an important consideration when evaluating design research. Specifically, is the formative evaluation plan sufficient for determining whether or not the design is moving toward better results and more insight at every stage in the design cycle? In particular, will the evaluation provide insight into why the design does or does not yield the desired results? It is this *why* question that is essential to good formative evaluation. In learning from design, it is critical to have a sense of why the design is leading to the outcomes that it is. Coupled with this formative evaluation, it is also helpful to have summary evaluation to limit risk in design research. Summary evaluation can answer the question, *Is this design approach showing enough promise to deserve to continue the design process?* Due to the innovative and exploratory nature of design research, we must be careful not to ask this question too early or too often, for fear of abandoning an innovative approach before it has been given time to reach its potential. Nevertheless, we must ask this question periodically and be willing to abandon an unsuccessful approach, having learned the lessons that arise from attempting it. This point about learning lessons from failed designs is important. In considering risk we must recognize that the failure of a design is not the failure of design research. When design research is conducted properly and systematically, just as many lessons can be learned from the design that fails as from one that achieves its goals.

Finally, in considering the design side of a design research proposal, it is important to apply the criteria one would use for any design or development proposal. These include: how appropriate is the proposed design approach for the problem or need? What expertise in design do the proposers bring? What is their previous experience with design?

Final thoughts: resources for design research

Design research offers the opportunity to create successful innovations and learn lessons that cannot be achieved through design and empirical research independently. In my opinion, this potential for gain outweighs the risk inherent in an exploratory research agenda. In this essay, I have focused on the considerations in assessing proposals for design research. However, there are other important questions regarding design research that remain to be addressed. For example, while I am able to say that good design research requires plans for research-driven design, systematic documentation, formative evaluation, and generalization, I must acknowledge that we lack accepted methods for developing and executing these plans. Each design research effort must essentially invent these methods itself. Similarly, I argue that design research teams must combine expertise in both design and research. However, it is not clear that we have the capacity to compose teams that combine these forms of expertise in existing educational institutions. Our expertise in educational design tends to be segregated from expertise in research. The former is locked up in institutions that have development responsibility and the latter in research institutions. In addition, we need to know how to integrate these forms of expertise as well as the practices of these two different communities if design research teams are to be successful. Finally, design research relies on a cooperative relationship between organizations that are responsible for the design and research and organizations that are responsible for implementation. The iterative design, development, implementation, and evaluation cycles that are critical for design research require long-term cooperative effort. These arrangements can be hard to maintain in an environment where those responsible for implementation are subject to demands for short-term results. An innovative design may require several iterations to reach its promise. In an atmosphere of short-term accountability, it may be hard to find implementation sites that can participate in this form of research. For all these reasons, the challenges of supporting design research go beyond the challenges of evaluating which research to pursue, to include significant challenges to existing human resources and institutional arrangements. Nevertheless, the possibility that substantial improvement in educational outcomes will result from innovative design research merits tackling those challenges.

Acknowledgment

This paper is based in part on research supported by the National Science Foundation under grants no. REC–9720663 and ESI–0227557. All opinions expressed here are those of the author and do not necessarily reflect the views of the Foundation.

References

Edelson, D. C. (2002). Design research: What we learn when we engage in design. *Journal of the Learning Sciences*, 11(1), 105–21.

van den Akker, J. (1999). Principles and methods of development research. In J. van den Akker, R. M. Branch, K. Gustafson, N. Nieveen, and T. Plomp (eds), *Design Approaches and Tools in Education and Training* (pp. 1–14). Boston: Kluwer Academic Publishers.

Chapter 8

Quality criteria for design research

Evidence and commitments

Anthony E. Kelly

Society devotes enormous effort to the education of children and adults. How to improve that effort via research is an ongoing challenge. Currently, researchers from fields as diverse as mathematics education, science education, computer science, and engineering are combining insights to forge a methodology that sits between the traditional randomized trials and qualitative approaches.

One set of these approaches is captured by the general label, *design research*. Design research is interventionist, iterative, process focused, collaborative, multilevel, utility oriented, and theory driven (Kelly 2003). It works with procedural ambiguity, ill-defined problems, and open systems that are socially multilevel, and multi-timescale (Lemke 2001).

Design research is often situated within a domain (for example, mathematics or science) and in many cases uses the structure of the domain as a theoretical guide (Cobb *et al.* 2003). Together with domain knowledge, design research uses a theory of social learning to pose and address "revisable conjectures" relevant to some "background theory" (Barab and Squire 2004).

Design research attempts to work within and holistically describe learning and teaching in spite of their complexity and local idiosyncrasy. Design research samples broadly and repeatedly from phenomena in addition to sampling theories or propositions in the literature.

Design research does not treat the educational process as some *black box* as randomized trials are wont to do, but embraces the complexity of learning and teaching and adopts an interventionist and *iterative* posture towards it. It uses ongoing *in situ* monitoring of the *failure or success* of (alternative versions of) some *designed artifact* (software, curricular intervention, tutoring session, etc.) to provide immediate (and accumulating) feedback on the viability of its "learning theory" or "hypothetical learning trajectory" (Cobb *et al.* 2003). Over time, the accumulating trail of evidence informs artifact redesign and theory revision.

Data collection often involves videotaping actual learning occurrences, the collection of "learning artifacts" (for example, students' work) and computer-tracked learning trails, and, in some cases, may involve other techniques such as clinical interviews or tutoring sessions (Kelly and Lesh 2000).

Design research seeks out, and is *responsive* to, emerging factors in complex, naturalistic settings and acknowledges the constraints and influence of the many nested layers impacting school practice from poverty to policy (Fishman *et al.* 2004).

In a preparatory document to the conference that shaped this book, Gravemeijer and van den Akker (2003) noted that there are at least three different uses for design research in education:

1 shaping an innovative intervention and developing a theory that underpins that intervention;
2 creating learning ecologies to investigate the possibilities for educational improvement by bringing about new forms of learning in order to study them; and
3 as a scientific approach to the design of educational interventions, aiming to contribute to design methodology.

Of these three, much attention in the United States of America has focused on the use of design principles to intervene in educational settings in what have traditionally been called "teaching experiments," but more recently, "design experiments." The design experiment does not describe a single methodology, since across these variants (Cobb *et al.* 2003; Kelly and Lesh 2000) exist differences in goals, methods, and measures:

- one-to-one teaching experiments;
- classroom teaching experiments (including multitiered and transformative versions);
- preservice teacher development studies;
- inservice teacher development studies; and
- school/district restructuring experiments.

As Gravemeijer and van den Akker noted, a second major emphasis is on the design and trials of "learning environments" (see Box 8.1 for examples). Within this subcategory, there also exist different goals, methods, and measures of learning or teaching or both.

As noted, further recent effort has been spent reflecting on the need to reconceptualize existing research methodologies or create new ones. Some notable efforts include the various articles in Kelly (2003), Barab and Kirshner (2001), and Barab and Squire (2004). Design research deliverables vary across many genres (Kelly 2003), and include the examples in Box 8.2.

The short review in Box 8.2 makes plain that a simple or single codification of criteria for judging the quality of *design research* studies or proposals is not plausible or even desirable. What I propose to do, instead, is to bracket

Box 8.1 Learning environment examples

- *Progress Portfolio*, Loh et al. (1998)
- *Worldwatcher*, Edelson et al. (1999)
- *LiteracyAccess Online*, Bannan-Ritland (2003)
- *Genscope/Biologica*, Hickey et al. (2003)
- *SimCalc*, Roschelle et al. (2000)
- *Jasper Series*, Cognition and Technology Group at Vanderbilt (1997)
- *WISE*, Linn et al. (2003)
- The various projects described at www.letus.org and www.cilt.org

Box 8.2 Genres in design research deliverables

- Reformulating the original research problem, iteratively, during research
- Explanatory frames or interpretive frameworks in future research efforts. For example, "ontological innovations" (ways of conceptualizing the complex milieu – "sociomathematical norms" or "meta-representational competence") and "theoretical constructs that empower us to see order, pattern, and regularity in complex settings" (diSessa and Cobb 2004: 84).
- Describing working models of practice
- Producing *local* or *humble* theory
- Establishing principles of design in complex social settings
- "Hypothetical learning trajectories" – proposed conceptual "pathways" employed by students and teachers navigating complex concepts
- Curricular materials ["Japanese Lesson Study" see http://www.lessonresearch.net/]
- Assessment task redesign (Kelly and Lesh 2000)
- Software and associated curricular supports (for example, *GenScope/Biologica*; *Worldwatcher*)
- "Learning environments" (for example, *WISE* and *TELS*, see www.telscenter.org)
- New or hybrid research methods (for example, Integrative Learning Design Framework – Bannan-Ritland 2003; McCandliss et al. 2003)
- Growth of a database of principles of research/artifact/"theory" design via video (Fuson and Zaritsky 2001)
- Use of a predesigned artifact (for example, a statistical display tool) to better understand process
- Learning from the act of designing an artifact as a *window* into learning (for example, *GenScope*)
- Putatively more "adoptable" products for teachers (Lagemann 2002a, 2002b, 2003)

the problem by returning to Brown's (1992) seminal article on design experiments. Brown did not simply propose a new method, rather:

- She advocated mixed methods approaches (qualitative *and* quantitative) in the same study: measuring magnitude of effects, yet also developing richer pictures of knowledge acquisition.
- She did not denounce quantitative measures; even for idiographic studies, she remarked, "it is perfectly possible to subject case studies to statistical analysis if one chose to do so" (Brown 1992: 156).
- She saw design research as involving classroom and laboratory *bi-directionality* (McCandliss *et al.* 2003).
- She recognized that overwhelming amounts of data would be collected, most of which would not be analyzed by researchers *and* peer reviewers due to time constraints.
- She warned against the "Bartlett Effect" of selecting episodes that supported one's favorite hypothesis. "This selection issue is nontrivial. The problem is how to avoid misrepresenting the data, however unintentionally" (Brown 1992: 162).
- She saw the need for dissemination (diffusion) studies: "[I]t is extremely important for the design experimenter to consider dissemination issues. It is *not sufficient* to argue that a reasonable end point is an existence proof, although this is indeed an important first step" (emphasis added, Brown (1992: 170)).
- She advocated scaling studies: "The alpha, or developmental, phase is under the control of the advocate, and by definition it must work for there to be any later phases. It works, though, under ideal supportive conditions. Next comes the beta phase, tryouts at carefully chosen sites with less, but still considerable, support. *Critical is the gamma stage*, widespread adoption with minimal support. If this stage is not attempted, the shelf life of any intervention must be called into question." (emphasis added, Brown (1992: 172)).
- Brown did *not* reject the goals of isolating variables and attributing causal impact. She recognized that to go to scale demands unconfounding the variables that were initially treated as confounded:

> I need to unconfound variables, not only for theoretical clarity, but also so that necessary and sufficient aspects of the intervention can be disseminated. The question becomes, what are the absolutely essential features that must be in place [for] ... normal school settings.
>
> (Brown 1992: 173)

- She did not provide a methodological solution for this problem, but suggested school system analyses and a study of the sociology of dissemination as sources.

We can now draw directly from Brown (1992) a set of concerns for the judging of the design and claims of design research in education:

- inadequate attention to sampling bias;
- inadequate attention to response bias;
- inadequate attention to researcher bias;
- overwhelming amounts of data and unsatisfactory methods of turning data into evidence;
- confounded variables;
- inadequate attention to scaling up or scaling out studies that test parameters outside the initial sample; and
- inadequate attention to dissemination and diffusion studies as tests of the efficacy of the emerging design *products*.

Brown's original concerns have not evaporated, recent sources documenting similar concerns include: Fishman *et al.* (2004), Barab and Kirshner (2001), and Shavelson *et al.* (2003).

It should be pointed out that the above problems not only afflict design research, but any research methods that attempt to model a phenomenon as complex as education. I do not see the above concerns about design research as invalidating the genre. Similar concerns became apparent in the development of correlational and experimental methods in psychology and education. A review of any current text on traditional experimental design will show a history of fixes and repair to the original work of Fisher in the early part of the twentieth century (Shadish *et al.* 2002). As with these other methods, we can expect, as a design research methodology matures, guidelines for researchers and journal editors on these concerns to emerge and be codified (Kelly *et al.* in preparation).

Commissive spaces in social science research

At the Dutch seminar that led to this book, I introduced the notion of a commissive space drawing on Searle's (1969) speech act theory, particularly the illocutionary/perlocutionary act of the commissive (that is, a commitment to act in accordance with certain background assumptions; see also Austin (1975)).

From this perspective, science as it is enacted socially is about commitments to certain assumptions that support specialized conversations within a peer group. Absent these conversations (which support the education and apprenticeship of new members), the various research methodological propositions in books and articles are merely ink on paper. Communities of practitioners develop shared commitments. These commitments – to background assumptions, acceptable verbal moves, adherence to standards of evidence, warrant, data, and technique – constitute the space in which research conversations can occur. Conversation here is viewed broadly as communications across many media and time via researcher training, professional presentations, articles, etc. Violations of the implicit and explicit commitments in the conversational space define the speaker as being outside of one commissive space and (presumably) a member of some other commissive space. Note that within a commissive space, it is often permissible to debate a finding (for example, disagreements about content, "is the p value significant?"), but not to question the foundational commitments.

To question a fundamental commitment (and sometimes even to make the background assumptions explicit) may cause the members of a commissive space to view the questioner as suspect. The questioner is assumed to be a member of some other commissive space. Other commissive spaces are judged somewhat foreign or inferior by dint of their existing outside of the research commitments of the exiling space. Note that this judgment is not made according to a set of background assumptions that encompass *both* commissive spaces; rather, that the questioner enunciated a position that violated the rejecting space's explicit or implicit rules and assumptions.

Pertinent to the current chapter, in educational research one commissive space is evidenced by a commitment to randomized field trials and assumes the analysis of *a posteriori* data in the light of *a priori* commitments to notions of sampling, sources of bias, the logic of experimental design, and inferential rules related to probability (Wainer and Robinson 2003; NRC 2002; Shavelson *et al.* 2003). In this space, it is preferable to conduct somewhat defective (quasi-experimental) randomized trials, rather than to question the putative model of causation assumed across all such trials.

Design researchers, in practice, violate many of the assumptions of the randomized field trials commissive space. Reiterating Brown (1992), Collins (1999) noted that a design researcher:

- conducts research in a messy (not lab) setting
- involves many dependent variables
- characterizes, but does not control, variables
- flexibly refines design rather than following a set of fixed procedures
- values social interaction over isolated learning
- generates profiles; does not test hypotheses
- values participant input to researcher judgments.

The point I want to make is that these violations of assumptions of the randomized field trials commissive space do not, necessarily, invalidate the scientific claims from the design research commissive space. To so argue is to reduce the human endeavor of science to its rare confirmatory studies. Rather, I wish to suggest that the commitments for conversations in both spaces are not fundamentally antagonistic, but can be seen as complementary in a more comprehensive view of the social sciences when directed at phenomena as complex education and learning.

To illustrate an antagonistic stance, consider that Shavelson *et al.* (2003) purportedly criticizing design research, focus their criticism almost exclusively on the narrative work of Bruner. As far as I know, Bruner does not see himself as a design researcher, nor do the design researchers I read base their work (at least centrally) on Bruner's ideas. Thus, the criticism is directed not against the particulars of design research in practice (whose complexity we see from the introduction). Rather, it is directed against design research's challenge to Shavelson *et al.*'s idea of what constitutes warrant for a research claim. In Shavelson *et al.*'s commissive space, assurance is best established by randomized field trials, which, presumably, are up to the task of ruling out rival hypotheses in complex educational settings (a claim I contest, NRC (2004)). Design research is, thus, suspect because it purportedly relies on Brunerian "narratives," which in their inability to rule out rival hypotheses (it is asserted) place the design research claims in doubt, and exile the methodology outside of the critics' commissive space.

Thus, I read the criticisms of Shavelson *et al.* (2003) of design research as understandable, but only within one set of commitments. Moreover, the assertion that randomized field trials stand as some kind of gold standard in educational research significantly narrows the enterprise of science and devalues processes and procedures known to support the generation of scientific knowledge (Holton 1998; Holton and Brush 2001) and is rejected by the more thoughtful users of randomized trials (Shadish *et al.* 2002).

The commissive space of design research

By comparison to the randomized field trials space, which is confirmatory and conservative, design research is exploratory and ambitious. Design research values novelty, and unconventional and creative approaches (Newell *et al.* 1962). Since design research perturbs and intervenes in learning or teaching situations (and thus primes unexpected behavior) it does not rely (solely) on existing frameworks of measures, but must provide solutions to modeling, sampling, and assessment problems as they emerge (Barab and Kirshner 2001).

Design research does not assume a mechanical (input/output) model of instruction and learning, but is more organic in its approach. It does not accept simple cause-and-effect models in complex social settings, so it does not centrally value the satisfaction of the establishment of internal validity.

Design research does not strive for *context-free* claims; rather, it sees context as central to its conceptual terrain. Its goal is to understand and foster meaning making and it sees this process as necessarily historical, cultural, and social. It thus does not seek to *randomize away* these influences (classifying them as "nuisance variables"), but to engage, understand, and influence them in an act of co-design with teachers and students around the learning of significant subject matter. Thus, design research is not concerned with isolating variables or making generalizable claims that arise from the satisfaction of techniques establishing external validity. It has an affinity with the methodological approaches in the personality theory of McAdams (1996, 1999, 2001), where the move is away from the "averaged" description of subjects – knowledge at the "level of the stranger" – to a more intimate definition of learning.

Design research is *experimental*, but not an experiment. It is hypothesis *generating* and *cultivating,* rather than *testing*; it is motivated by emerging conjectures. It involves blueprinting, creation, intervention, trouble-shooting, patching, repair; reflection, retrospection, reformulation, and reintervention. Design research promotes a dialectic between direct empirical observation, videotaped records, co-researchers' commentary and the design researcher's own fundamental understanding (models) of the subject matter, students' and teachers' emerging models of the subject matter (and, in some cases, models of the social classroom milieu). Thus, the multifactor *expertise* of the researcher(s) and the commitment and engagement of the *subjects* is paramount.

Design research may be seen as a *stage-appropriate response* in a multistage *program* of research that moves from speculation, to observation, to identification of variables and processes via prototyping, to models and more definitive testing of those models, to implementation studies, scaling studies, and ongoing diffusion of innovations (Bannan-Ritland 2003). Thus, design research may lead to, support, and enrich randomized field trials. Indeed, the findings of a randomized trials study may be incorporated into the *theory* being tested in design research.

Design researchers choose to work in the "context of discovery" rather than in the "context of verification" (Schickore and Steinle 2002). Thus, in areas in which little is known (for example, how to teach and how students learn statistics), exploratory or descriptive work naturally precedes (and informs) randomized field trials, which, incidentally, are meaningless without this foundational work. What variables should be controlled for or measured if the phenomenon is not well understood? Design research may be seen as contributing to model formulation "meaningfulness" (not yet estimation or validation (Sloane and Gorard 2003), not (yet) "demarcation" (Kelly 2004)). Ultimately, the use of design research methods is a *point of entry* choice on the researcher's part – where in the cycle of observation/correlation/experimentation to engage.

On the other hand, while it is a category error to *arbitrarily* impose the adjudicative criteria of one commissive community upon the other, if claims pertinent to a different space are made, then the criteria of the other space are relevant. Thus, if researchers make strong causal claims using only the methods of design research, these claims can and should be met with the force of the argumentative grammar of the randomized field trials' commissive space (Kelly 2004). Conversely, unless significant multiple or mixed methods are adopted in randomized field trials (Shadish *et al.* 2002), statements beyond black box process models equally trespass on the conceptual train of design research and other commissive spaces in educational research.

Moving forward

Design research should pay greater attention to advances in mixed methods (Mosteller and Boruch 2002; Shadish *et al.* 2002) and more expansive views of randomized field trials (Dietrich and Markman 2000; O'Donnell 2000; Tashakkori and Teddlie 2000). In particular, since design research focuses on learning, it must consider the basis for choosing one and abandoning other potential design directions in light of revised models of transfer (Lobato 2003). Perspectives on transfer are also key for generalizability tests of any models that arise from design research data.

Design research should advance over time from model formulation to estimation and validation (Sloane and Gorard 2003). Proponents should continue to lead in developing new approaches for video use and analysis: for example, the CILT work (www.cilt.org/seedgrants/community/Pea_Final_Report_2002.pdf, and Diver (www.stanford.edu/~roypea/HTML1%20Folder/DIVER.html). Incidentally, there are many innovative approaches to data collection and analyses at the National Science Digital Library project (http://nsdl.org/).

Design researchers need to continue to temper strong causal claims and be clear about the character of their claims and their appropriate evidence and warrant (Kelly 2004; NRC 2002). In some cases, it may be feasible and productive to conduct mini randomized trials at choice points and consider actor-oriented perspectives on learning at key junctures.

Design research should continue to explore models for the diffusion of innovations (Rogers 2003), so that the deliverables of design research are used within the research, policy, and practice fields. Equally, it should explore models for scaling successful innovations (www.gse.harvard.edu/scalingup/sessions/websum.htm and http://drdc.uchicago.edu/csu/index.shtml).

Since design research is emerging as a new approach to research in applied settings, it is important to recognize its growing appeal. I wish to recognize the support received from the National Science Foundation for a grant to me and Richard Lesh (University of Indiana, Bloomington) on explicating this emerging method. This grant has supported and documented a significant international co-emerging interest in the role of design in educational research. These meetings led to the special issue of the *Educational Researcher* (Kelly 2003), and an upcoming book on design research (Kelly *et al.* in preparation).

Additionally, I have learned of spontaneous examples of design-based research methods during visits to the United Kingdom (particularly speaking to researchers associated with the Economic and Social Research Council's

(ESRC's) Teaching and Learning Research Programme – www.tlrp.org – and Oxford University), Sweden (Gothenburg University, particularly the Learning Study method of the Marton group), the Learning Lab in Denmark, the Center for Research in Pedagogy and Practice in Singapore, and, of course, the NWO and PROO in the Netherlands. My hope is that the creative efforts of design researchers continue to be supported and that these efforts are not prematurely derailed by perceived violations of certain commissive spaces (Asch 1966). The methodological work of the next decade should include the articulation and strengthening of the various research commissive spaces that span the program of research from innovation, to diffusion, to societal consequences (Bannan-Ritland 2003).

References

Asch, S. E. (1966). Opinions and social pressure. In A. P. Hare, E. F. Borgatta, and R. F. Bales (eds), *Small Groups: Studies in Social Interaction* (pp. 318–24). New York: Alfred A. Knopf.

Austin, J. L. (1975). *How to Do Things With Words* (second edition) (J. O. Urmson and Marina Sbisà (eds)). Cambridge, MA: Harvard University Press..

Bannan-Ritland, B. (2003). The role of design in research: The integrative learning design framework. *Educational Researcher, 32*(1), 21–4.

Barab, S. and Kirshner, D. (2001). Rethinking methodology in the learning sciences [Special issue]. *Journal of the Learning Sciences, 10*(1–2), 5–15.

Barab, S. A. and Squire, K. (2004). Design-based research: Clarifying the terms [Special issue]. *Journal of the Learning Sciences, 13*(1).

Brown, A. L. (1992). Design experiments: Theoretical and methodological challenges in creating complex interventions in classroom settings. *Journal of the Learning Sciences, 2*, 141–78.

Cobb, P., Confrey, J., diSessa, A., Lehrer, R., and Schauble, L. (2003). Design experiments in educational research. *Educational Researcher, 32*(1), 9–13.

Cognition and Technology Group at Vanderbilt (1997). *The Jasper Project: Lessons in Curriculum, Instruction, Assessment, and Professional Development.* Mahwah, NJ: Erlbaum.

Collins, A. (1999). The changing infrastructure of education research. In E. Lagemann and L. Shulman (eds), *Issues in Education Research* (pp. 289–98). San Francisco: Jossey-Bass.

Dietrich, E. and Markman, A. B. (eds) (2000). *Cognitive Dynamics: Conceptual and Representational Change in Humans and Machines.* Mahwah, NJ: Erlbaum.

diSessa, A. and Cobb, P. (2004). Ontological innovation and the role of theory in design experiments. *Journal of the Learning Sciences, 13*(1), 77–103.

Edelson, D. C., Gordin, D. N., and Pea, R. D. (1999). Addressing the challenges of inquiry-based learning through technology and curriculum design. *Journal of the Learning Sciences, 8*(3/4), 391–450.

Fishman, B., Marx, R., Blumenfeld, P., and Krajcik, J. (2004). Creating a framework for research on systemic technology innovations. *Journal of the Learning Sciences.*

Fuson, K. and Zaritsky, R. A. (2001). *Children's Math Worlds* (DVD Multi Audio and Video Tracks, Interactive). Evanston, IL: NSF Grant.

Gravemeijer, K. and van den Akker, J. (2003, December). *How to review proposals for design research?* Working document for the PROO workshop, Amsterdam.

Hickey, D. T., Kindfield, A. C. H., Horwitz, P., and Christie, M. A. (2003). Integrating curriculum, instruction, assessment, and evaluation in a technology-supported genetics environment. *American Educational Research Journal, 40*(2), 495–538.

Holton, G. (1998). *Scientific Imagination.* Cambridge, MA: Harvard University Press.

Holton, G. and Brush, S. G. (2001). *Physics, the Human Adventure: From Copernicus to Einstein and Beyond.* New Brunswick, NJ: Rutgers University Press.

Kelly, A. E. (2003). Research as design. Theme issue: The role of design in educational research. *Educational Researcher, 32*(1), 3–4.

Kelly, A. E. (2004). Design research in education: Yes, but is it methodological? *Journal of the Learning Sciences, 13*(1), 115–28.

Kelly, A. E. and Lesh, R. (eds) (2000). *Handbook of Research Design in Mathematics and Science Education.* Mahwah, NJ: Erlbaum.

Kelly, A. E., Lesh, R., and Baek, J. (eds) (in preparation). *Handbook of Design Research Methods in Mathematics, Science and Technology Education.* Mahwah, NJ: Erlbaum.

Lagemann, E. (2002a). *An Elusive Science: The Troubling History of Education Research.* Chicago: Chicago University Press.

Lagemann, E. (2002b). *Usable knowledge in education.* A memorandum for the Spencer Foundation Board of Directors. www.spencer.org/publications/usable_knowledge_report_ecl_a.htm

Lagemann, E. (2003). *Aiming for usability.* http://www.gse.harvard.edu/news/features/lagemann03202003.html

Lemke, J. L. (2001). The long and the short of it: Comments on multiple timescale studies of human activity. *Journal of the Learning Sciences, 10*(1–2),17–26.

Linn, M. C., Davis, E. A., and Bell, P. (2003). *Internet Environments for Science Education.* Mahwah, NJ: Erlbaum.

Lobato, J. (2003). How design experiments can inform a rethinking of transfer and vice versa. *Educational Researcher, 32*(1), 17–20.

Loh, B., Radinsky, J., Russell, E., Gomez, L. M., Reiser, B. J., and Edelson, D. C. (1998). The progress portfolio: Designing reflective tools for a classroom context. In *Proceedings of CHI 98* (pp. 627–34). Reading, MA: Addison-Wesley.

McAdams, D. P. (1996). Personality, modernity, and the storied self: A contemporary framework for studying persons. *Psychological Inquiry, 7*, 295–321.

McAdams, D. P. (1999). Personal narratives and the life story. In L. Pervin, and O. John (eds), *Handbook of Personality: Theory and Research* (second edition) (pp. 478–500). New York: Guilford Press.

McAdams, D. P. (2001). The psychology of life stories. *Review of General Psychology, 5*, 100–22.

McCandliss, P. D., Kalchman, M., and Bryant, P. (2003). Design experiments and laboratory approaches to learning: Steps toward collaborative exchange. *Educational Researcher, 32*(1), 14–16.

Mosteller, F. and Boruch. R. (eds) (2002) *Evidence Matters: Randomized Trials in Educational Research.* Washington, DC: Brookings Institution.

Newell, A., Shaw, J. C., Simon, H. A. (1962). The process of creative thinking. In H.

F. Gruber and W. Wertheimer (eds), *Contemporary Approaches to Creative Thinking* (pp. 63–119). New York: Atherton Press.

NRC (National Research Council) (2002) In Shavelson, R. J. and Towne, L. (eds), *Scientific Research in Education*. Washington, DC: National Academies Press.

NRC (National Research Council) (2004) Committee on Research in Education. In L. Towne, L. L. Wise, and T. M. Winters (eds), *Advancing Scientific Research in Education*. Washington, DC: National Academies Press.

O'Donnell, A. M. (ed.) (2000). Learning with peers: Multiple perspectives on collaboration. *The Journal of Experimental Education*, 69(1).

Rogers, E. (2003). *Diffusion of Innovations*. New York: Free Press.

Roschelle, J., Kaput, J., and Stroup, W. (2000). SimCalc: Accelerating students' engagement with the mathematics of change. In M. Jacobson and R. Kozma (eds), *Educational Technology and Mathematics and Science for the 21st Century* (pp. 47–75). Mahwah, NJ: Erlbaum.

Schickore, J. and Steinle, F. (eds) (2002). *Revisiting Discovery and Justification*. Preprint 211. Berlin: Max Planck Institute for History of Science.

Searle, J. (1969). *Speech Acts: An Essay in the Philosophy of Language*. Cambridge: Cambridge University Press.

Shadish, W. R., Cook, T. D., and Campbell, D. T. (2002). *Experimental and Quasi-Experimental Designs for Generalized Causal Inference*. Boston: Houghton Mifflin.

Shavelson, R. J., Phillips, D. C., Towne, L., and Feuer, M. J. (2003). On the science of education design studies. *Educational Researcher*, 32(1), 25–8.

Sloane, F. C. and Gorard, S. (2003). Exploring modeling aspects of design experiments. *Educational Researcher*, 32(1), 29–31.

Tashakkori, A. and Teddlie, C. (eds). (2000), *Handbook of Mixed Methods in Social and Behavioral Research*. Thousand Oaks, CA: Sage Publications.

Wainer, H. and Robinson, D. H. (2003). Shaping up the practice of null hypothesis significance testing. *Educational Researcher*, 32(7), 22–30.

Part 4

Moving ahead

Chapter 9

From design research to large-scale impact

Engineering research in education

Hugh Burkhardt

Introduction

Previous chapters have described the current state of design research and its future prospects, setting out its contribution in bringing research in education closer to what actually happens in classrooms. Indeed, the last 30 years have been remarkable for the shift from the traditional combination of critical commentary on the one hand and laboratory experiments on the other, towards the empirical study of teachers and children in real classrooms. The growth of cognitive science and its application to research in more realistic learning environments has contributed much to this. The establishment of design research over the last decade represents the next step in this sequence. However, there is more to be done before teaching and learning *in the majority of classrooms* can possibly move to being research-based. How we may get there, and the progress so far, is the theme of this chapter.

First, we need an established research-based methodology for taking the design research approach forward to produce processes and tools that work well in practice with teachers and students who are typical of the target groups. I shall argue that this methodology is already in place, and describe how it works. This research approach is characteristic of engineering disciplines, with *new or better products and processes* as the primary outcomes, so we call it the *engineering research* approach.[1] Direct *impact* on practice is the main criterion of quality, though engineering research also delivers new *insights* – and journal articles. Second, we need reliable models of the process of educational change. These we do not yet have. I will outline progress that has been made, giving reasonable hope that a research-based developmental approach can succeed here too.

In what follows, we first begin with a comparison of the traditional *craft-based* approach to the improvement of professional practice with the *research-based* approach, going on to outline the key elements in the latter and how various groups contribute to it. The section that follows discusses the research infrastructure in education, the contributions of different research traditions to it, and the increased proportion of engineering research needed for the development of new and improved products and processes – and, through this, for impact on policy and practice. The next section describes the process of design, development and evaluation that is characteristic of this engineering research approach.

In the next two sections, we then discuss how one can build the skill base needed for such a program and analyse the implications for governments, industry and academia. The penultimate section sketches an answer to the question *How much would good engineering cost?*, while the final section summarizes the implications of all this for policy and for the design and development community. This wide-ranging agenda inevitably limits the detail in which the analysis can be justified, or exemplified; the still-too-limited evidence is thus mainly listed in the references.

R↔P: Research-based improvement of professional practice

Educational research still has much less impact on policy and practice than we would wish. If politicians have a problem in their education system, is their first move to call a research expert? Not often. Indeed, in most countries, there is no obvious link between changes in practice and any of the research of the tens of thousands of university researchers in education around the world. It is not like that in more research-based fields like medicine or engineering. Let us try to identify why.

Craft-based versus research-based approaches

I shall use two contrasting terms for improvement methodologies, *craft-based* and *research-based*. Like most dichotomies, it is an over-simplification but, I believe, useful.

In all professional fields, there is recognized *good practice*, embodying the established *craft skills* of the field. These are based on the collective experience of practitioners – they must always have a response to every situation that presents itself, whether they are teachers in a classroom, doctors in a surgery, or administrators running a system. Experienced professionals pass on good practices, and the skills involved, to new entrants in their training. This is what I mean by the *craft-based approach*. Historically, it was the approach of the craft *guilds* including, among many others, doctors and teachers. In this approach, innovation comes from a few people pushing the boundaries of good practice, trying something new and seeing if it works – for them. This sometimes involves the invention of new tools – instruments, teaching materials, etc. Others learn about it, and some try it; on the basis of this experience, they decide whether or not to adopt the innovation. If many take it up, it gradually becomes part of *good practice* – even then, it may be adopted by only a small minority of the profession.

All fields start with this approach, which has its strengths and limitations. It is inexpensive and anyone can take part. However, in judging an innovation, it lacks systematic evaluation of effectiveness in well-defined circumstances: for who, what, and when, does it *work*, and with what range of outcomes? Furthermore, it inevitably depends on the extrapolation of current experience in a *clinical* context; since any extrapolation is inherently unreliable, such exploration tends to be limited in scope.

Thus, the craft-based approach to innovation is limited in the range of possibilities it explores, and in the reliability of its conclusions. This has led to the search for more powerful and systematic, research-based approaches in many fields. Millennia ago, engineering took the lead in this. Starting in the late nineteenth century, medicine began to follow. Education set out on this path in the twentieth century. Other fields are also instructive. The clothing industry remains firmly craft-based, with changes driven by changes in fashion – hemlines go up and down, just as educational fashion swings back and forth between *basic skills* and *problem solving*; however, performance clothing for campers, climbers or astronauts is substantially research-based, and even has useful influence on some areas of fashion. For education, medicine seems a better model than the fashion industry.

Research-based approaches to improvement in large-scale educational practice are the theme of this chapter. Here it will suffice to say that its methods aim to:

- build on results from past research, as well as best practice;
- use research methods in a systematic process of exploring possibilities; then
- develop tools and processes for their use through creative design and successive refinement based on using research methods to get rich, detailed feedback in well-specified circumstances.

This is inevitably a slower and more costly approach than craft-based innovation. Slowly, over many years, research-based innovations gradually make an increasing contribution to the quality of practice in a field. Engineering is now largely research-based – bridges, aeroplanes and other products are designed from well-established theories and the known properties of materials. Over the last century, medicine has moved from being entirely craft-based to being substantially research-based. Fundamental discoveries, particularly in molecular biology, as well as a huge research effort have accelerated that process. Many treatments, in areas from the common cold to low-back pain, are still largely craft-based. Alternative/complementary medicine is almost entirely craft-based. However, the areas that have the firmer foundations of the research-based approach gradually expand. Education has only begun to move in this direction; nonetheless, progress has been made and is being made in both methodology and outcomes. What follows outlines some of it.

Key elements for research-based improvement

In a recent paper on 'Improving educational research' (Burkhardt and Schoenfeld (2003), referred to here as *IER*), we described the elements of R↔P mechanisms that are common to successful research-based fields of professional practice such as medicine and the design and engineering of consumer electronics. They all have robust mechanisms for taking ideas from laboratory scale to widely used practice. Such mechanisms typically involve multiple inputs from established research, the imaginative design of prototypes, refinement on the basis of feedback from systematic development, and marketing mechanisms that rely in part on respected third party in-depth evaluations. These lab-to-engineering-to-marketing linkages typically involve the academic community and a strong research-active industry (for example, the drug companies, Bell Labs, Xerox PARC, IBM and Google).

The following elements are all important in achieving effective and robust products:

- A body of reliable research, with a reasonably stable theoretical base, a minimum of faddishness and *a clear view of the reliable range of each aspect of the theory.* This in turn requires norms for research methods and reporting that are rigorous and consistent, resulting in a set of insights and/or prototype tools on which designers can rely. The goal, achieved in other fields, is *cumulativity* – a growing core of results, developed through studies that build on previous work, which are accepted by both the research community and the public as reliable and non-controversial within a well-defined range of circumstances. Such a theory base allows for a clear focus on important issues and provides sound (though still limited) guidance for the design of improved solutions to important problems.
- Stable design teams of adequate size to grapple with large tasks over the relatively long time scales required for sound work of major importance in both research and development. Informed by the research base and good practice, they add another crucial ingredient – design skill, even brilliance.
- Systematic iterative development that takes the tools through successive rounds of trials and revision in increasingly realistic circumstances of use and users.
- Independent comparative in-depth evaluation provides validation (or not): Do they work as claimed, in the range of circumstances claimed? This provides the basis for the following point.
- Individual and group accountability for ideas and products, so that reputations are built on a track record of evidence.

It should be clear that this approach requires ongoing development programs on realistic time scales, funded by clients who understand the process. To do it well needs substantial teams; it cannot be done by individual researchers in a few years – the normal circumstances of university research in education.

Around the world there are some well-established high-quality engineering research groups – EDC, TERC and COMAP are notable U.S. examples; however, these and most other groups work from project to project, with no continuity of funding or, consequently, of work. Only the Freudenthal Institute has had a substantial team (now about 70 people), supported by continuing funding from the Netherlands Government over many decades;[2] the quality of their work on basic research, design and engineering is universally recognized – and reflected in the performance of the Netherlands in international comparison tests in mathematics. It represents the best current exemplar for governments elsewhere to study.

Key contributors – roles and barriers

In this approach, who are the key players, what are their roles, and current barriers to the fulfilment of these roles?

Client funders, as well as providing the money that supports the work, should be partners in goal and product definition through a continuing process of negotiation that reconciles their goals and design constraints in the best solution that can be devised; the main barriers to this are often an unquestioned acceptance of the traditional craft-based approach, left undisturbed by the lack of comparative in-depth evaluation of the effectiveness of products, or an insistence on 'simple solutions' that will not, in practice, meet their goals.

Project leaders guide the strategic planning and ongoing direction of their team's work. This involves negotiation with funders, and process management at all levels from design to marketing. The main barriers to project leaders' development are the lack of continuity produced by one-off project funding, and the consequent absence of a career path for engineering researchers – that is, systems for training and apprenticeship, appointment and promotion, and recognition.

A *designer/developer* provides excellence in design, and refinement through feedback from trials; the main barriers are, again, the lack of any career path for designers or the in-depth evaluation that would enable the recognition of excellence in design.

Insight-focused researchers build the reliable research base, and carry out the comparative in-depth evaluation, both formative and summative, of products, which is so important; the main barrier is the academic system, which undervalues such project-focused work, and also contributes to the other barriers above.

Each group needs to play these vital roles. In the section 'Changing behaviour in academia, industry, governments' (p. 142) we look at the changes that are needed in their current working environments to make this possible.

The research infrastructure – insight versus impact as research goals

At a fundamental level, the relative impotence of research in education arises from the interaction of different research traditions and styles, characteristic respectively of the humanities, sciences, engineering and the arts. For this analysis, we need to go beyond the familiar controversies and *paradigm wars* in education; well-organized fields recognize that strength in research requires a wide range of approaches, tailored to the problems at hand. Let us take a broader view, looking across fields at the four characteristic research styles and asking how each contributes to education. For this, it is useful to have a definition of research (HEFC 1999), designed to cover all fields:[3]

> 'Research' is to be understood as original investigation undertaken in order to gain knowledge and understanding. It includes work of direct relevance to the needs of commerce and industry, as well as to the public and voluntary sectors; scholarship; the invention and generation of ideas and, images, performances and artifacts including design, where these lead to new or substantially improved insights; and the use of existing knowledge in experimental development to produce new or substantially improved materials, devices, products and processes, including design and construction.
>
> (RAE 2001)

If you then look for a fundamental measure of *quality* in research across all fields, it is difficult to go beyond *impressing key people in your field* – but the balance of qualities that achieves this varies from field to field. What balance would be most beneficial for education, and how well is it reflected in current criteria for excellence in research? Let us look at each style in turn, the nature of the activities, the forms of output and, in context of education, the potential impact on students' learning in typical classrooms.

The humanities *approach*

This is the oldest research tradition, summarized in the aforementioned RAE (2001) exercise as 'original investigation undertaken in order to gain knowledge and understanding; scholarship; the invention and generation of ideas ... where these lead to new or substantially improved insights.' Empirical testing of the assertions made is *not* involved. The key product is *critical commentary*, usually published in single-author books, journal papers or, indeed, journalism.

There is a lot of this in education, partly because anyone can play at making assertions, expert or not; indeed, there is no popular acceptance of expertise. The ideas and analysis in the best work of this kind, based on the authors' observation and reflections on their experience, are valuable. Without the requirement of further empirical testing, a great deal of ground can be covered. However, since so many plausible ideas in education have not worked in practice, the lack of empirical support is a major weakness. How can you distinguish reliable comment from plausible speculation? This has led to a search for *evidence-based education*.

The science *approach*

This approach to research is also focused on the development of better *insights* and improved understanding of *how the world works* through the analysis of phenomena and the building of models which explain them, but in this case it includes the *empirical testing of those models*. This last is the essential difference from the humanities approach – the assertions made, now called hypotheses or models, depend on rigorous empirical testing for credibility. The main products are: *assertions with evidence-based arguments in support*, including *evidence-based responses to key questions*. The evidence must be empirical, and presented in a form that could be replicated. The products are conference talks and journal papers.

Schoenfeld (2002) has suggested three dimensions for classifying research outputs:

- Generalizability: To how wide a set of circumstances is the statement claimed to apply?
- Trustworthiness: How well substantiated are the claims?
- Importance: How much should we care?

Typically, any given paper contains assertions in different parts of this three-dimensional space. Importance, a key variable, could usefully distinguish *insight* from *impact*. Figure 9.1 focuses on the other two variables, G and T, say. A typical research study looks carefully at a particular situation, perhaps a specific treatment and student responses to it. The results are high on T, low on G – zone A in the figure. Typically, the conclusions section of the paper goes on to discuss the *implications* of the study, often much more wide-ranging but with little evidence to support the generalizations made, which are essentially speculative (in the humanities tradition) – shown as X, Y and Z.

A lot of research really provides evidence *on treatments, not on the principles* the authors claim to study; to probe the latter, one needs evidence on

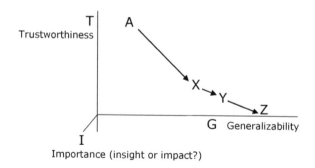

Figure 9.1   Graphical representation of typical study outputs (based on Schoenfeld 2002)

generalizability – one must check stability across a range of variables (student, teacher, designer and topic). Only substantial studies, or sometimes meta-analyses, can meet this need. The 'Diagnostic teaching' work of Alan Bell, Malcolm Swan and others illustrate this. The approach is based on leading students whose conceptual understanding is not yet robust into making errors, then helping them understand and debug them through discussion – see, for example, Bell (1993). Their first study compared a diagnostic teaching treatment to a standard 'positive only' teaching approach. It showed similar learning gains through the teaching period (pre- to post-test) but without the fall away over the following 6 months that the comparison group showed. This study was for *one mathematics topic*, with the detailed treatment designed by *one designer*, taught by *one teacher* to *one class*. Only five years later, when the effect was shown to be stable across many topics, designers, teachers and classes could one begin to make reasonably trustworthy statements about diagnostic teaching as an approach. Few studies persist in this way. Even then, further questions will remain – in this case, as so often, about how well *typical* teachers in realistic circumstances of support will handle diagnostic teaching. Work on this continues.

My general point is that insight-focused research with adequate evidence on its range of validity needs time and teams beyond the scale of an individual Ph.D. or research grant. Other academic subjects, from molecular biology to high-energy physics, arrange this; if it were more common in education, the research could have high G *and* T and, if the importance were enough, be worth the serious attention of designers and policymakers.

There is the further issue of grain size. Studies of student learning in tightly controlled laboratory conditions are too artificial to use directly in guiding design for the classroom. At the other extreme, studies of student performance on complete programs tell you little about the classroom causes. Design research addresses the key problems directly.

The science approach is now predominant in research in science and mathematics education; it is not yet influential in policy formation. Such research provides insights, identifies problems and suggests possible ways forward. Design research takes this one step further into more realistic learning environments; it does not itself generate *practical solutions for situations that are typical of the system* – that also needs good engineering.

The engineering *approach*

This approach aims to go beyond improved insights to direct practical *impact* – helping the world *to work better* by, not only understanding how it works, but developing *robust* solutions to recognized practical problems. It builds on science insights, insofar as they are available, but goes beyond them. Within the broad RAE (2001) definition mentioned previously it is *"the invention and generation of ideas ... and the use of existing knowledge in experimental development to produce new or substantially improved materials, devices, products and processes, including design and construction."* Again there is an essential requirement for the empirical testing of products and processes, both formatively in the development process and in evaluation. The key products are: *tools and/or processes that work well for their intended uses and users; evidence-based evaluation and justification; responses to evaluation questions.* When, and only when, it includes these elements, is development engineering research.

This approach is still uncommon in education – though there are many good examples, it is not the way most challenges are tackled.[4] In the academic education community such work is often undervalued – in many places only insight-focused research in the science tradition is regarded as true research currency. In this environment, it is not surprising that most design research stresses the new insights it provides rather than the products and processes it has developed, even though these could be valuable if developed further. The effects of the current low academic status of educational engineering include:

- lower standards of materials and processes, since the imaginative design and rigorous development that good engineering requires are not widely demanded;
- lower practical impact of important results from insight-focused research, since designers feel less need to know or use this research; and
- pressure on academics in universities to produce insight research papers, rather than use engineering research methods. (These could also be used to improve their own practice, both in effectiveness and transferability to others.)

All this leaves a hiatus between insight-focused research and improved classroom practice, which is unfortunate. Society's priorities for education are mainly practical – that young people should learn to function in life as effectively as possible, including the personal satisfaction and growth that good education provides. The failure of educational research to deliver in practical terms is reflected in the low levels of financial support for it.

The arts approach

A change in the criteria of excellence in fine arts is noteworthy. Fifty years ago, only critics and historians of art or music would be appointed to senior academic positions; now active artists, painters and composers, are appointed – as are designers and innovative practitioners in engineering and medicine. This may be seen as related to the humanities approach rather as engineering is to the science approach. It reminds us that design is more than the routine application of a set of scientific principles. (Indeed, the finest engineering, from the Porsche to the iPod, has a strong aesthetic aspect.) It enriches education and could do more.

Integrating the traditions

In summary, let me stress that this is far from a plea for the abandonment of insight-focused science research in education, or even the critical commentary of the humanities tradition; these are essential, *but not nearly enough*. Rather, it is an argument about balance – that there should be much more impact-focused engineering research and that it should receive comparable recognition and reward. *The different styles can and should be complementary and mutually supportive.* But more engineering research is essential if impact is to be a research priority of the field. As we deliver impact, our work will become more useful to practice, more influential on policy – and, as other fields have shown, much better funded.

The status and roles of theory

Finally, some related comments on *theory*, seen as the key mark of quality in educational research as in most fields. I am strongly in favour of theory. (Indeed, in my other life, I am a theoretical physicist.) However, in assessing its role, it is crucial to be clear as to how *strong* the theory is. From a practical point of view, the key question is: *how far is current theory an adequate basis for design?*

A strong theory provides an explanation of what is behind an array of observations. It is complete enough to model the behaviour it explains, to predict outputs from conditions and inputs. In fields like aeronautical engineering, the theory is strong; the model is complete enough to handle nearly all the relevant variables so that those who know the theory can design an aeroplane at a computer, build it, and it will fly, and fly efficiently. (They still flight test it extensively and exhaustively.) In medicine, theory is moderately weak, so that trial design and testing is more central. Despite all that is known about physiology and pharmacology, much development is not theory-driven. The development of new drugs, for example, is still mainly done by testing the effects of very large numbers of naturally occurring substances; they are chosen intelligently, based on analogy with known drugs, but the effects are not predictable and the search is wide. However, as fundamental work on DNA has advanced, and with it the theoretical under-standing of biological processes, designer drugs with much more theoretical input have begun to be developed. This process will continue. Looking across fields, it seems that the power of theory and the engineering research approach develop in parallel.

Education is a long way behind medicine, let alone engineering, in the range and reliability of its theories. By overestimating their strength, damage has been done to children – for example, by designing curricula based largely on behaviourist theories. It is not that behaviourism, or constructivism, is wrong; indeed, they are both right in their core ideas but they are *incomplete* and, on their own, make an inadequate basis for design. Physicists would call them 'effects'. The harm comes from overestimating their power.

Let me illustrate this with an example from meteorology. 'Air flows from regions of high pressure to regions of low pressure' sounds like and is good physics. It implies that air will come out of a popped balloon or a pump. It also implies that winds should blow perpendicular to the isobars, the contour lines of equal pressure on a weather map, just as water flows downhill, *perpendicular* to the contour lines of a slope. However, a look at a good weather map in England shows that the winds are closer to *parallel* to the isobars. That is because *there is another effect*, the Coriolis effect. It is due to the rotation of the earth which 'twists' the winds in a subtle way, anticlockwise around low pressure regions (in the northern hemisphere). There are many such effects operating in education but, as in economics, it is impossible to predict just how they will balance out in a given situation. Thus, design skill and empirical development are essential, with theoretical input providing useful heuristic guidance. The essential point is that *the design details matter* – they have important effects on outcomes and are guided, not determined, by theory.[5]

This paper is about how to achieve educational goals. I will not explicitly discuss the goals themselves. This is only partly because the subject is huge and disputatious. I believe that, in mathematics and science at least, many of the apparently goal-focused disputes are in fact based on strongly held beliefs about how to achieve them, some of which fly in the face of the research evidence. For example, those who think mathematics should focus on procedural 'basic skills' in arithmetic and algebra usually want students to be able to solve real-world problems with mathematics, but think 'they must have a firm foundation of skills first.' It is true that some with a strong faith-based world view believe that schools should not encourage students to question authority – an essential aspect of problem solving and investigation; however, even here, the greater challenge is to equip teachers to handle investigative work in their classroom. There is, therefore, an implicit assumption here that the educational goals we address are those that research on learning and teaching suggest are essential – a challenging enough set.

Systematic design, development and evaluation

From this analysis of framework and infrastructure, it is time to move on to look in more detail at engineering research itself – the methodology that enables it to produce high-quality tools, with processes for their effective use. The approach is based on a fusion of the elements already discussed:

- research input from earlier research and development worldwide;
- design skill, led by designers who have produced exceptional materials;
- co-development with members of the target communities;
- rich, detailed feedback from successive rounds of developmental trials to guide revision of the materials, so that intentions and outcomes converge; and
- a well-defined locus of 'design control', so that wide consultation can be combined with design coherence.

Typically, there are three stages: design, systematic development and evaluation. I discuss each in turn, with brief exemplification from one project. Research of various kinds plays several roles: input to design from earlier research; research methods for the development process; in-depth research for evaluation, to inform users on product selection and the design community on future development.

The example I shall use is from the (still ongoing) development of support for *mathematical literacy*, now called *functional mathematics* in England. Our work began in the 1980s with a project called *Numeracy Through Problem Solving* (NTPS; Shell Centre 1987–89). U.K. Government interest has recently revived (Tomlinson Report 2004), partly through the emergence of PISA (OECD 2003) and (yet again) of employers' concern at the non-functionality of their employees' mathematics.

Design

The importance of sound design principles, based on the best insight research, has long been clear. They are necessary but not sufficient for the production of excellent tools for practitioners, essentially because of our current far-from-complete understanding of learning and teaching. The other key factor is excellence in design; it makes the difference between an acceptable-but-mediocre product and one that is outstanding, empowering the users and lifting their spirits.

Excellent design is balanced across the educational goals, covering both functional effectiveness and aesthetic attractiveness. (Porsches are the wonderful cars they are because they're classy *and* superbly engineered. There are sleek-looking cars one wouldn't want to own, for very long at least.) As in every field, design that is aimed at superficial aspects of the product (textbooks in 4-color editions, with lots of sidebars with historical and other trivia, pictures that have no connection with the topic, etc.) at the expense of effectiveness (in promoting learning) is poor educational design. (Focused on increasing sales rather than increasing student understanding, they may be good *business* design.)

In the humanities and the arts, teachers can build their lessons around outstanding works – of literature or music, for example, in their infinite variety. Because the learning focus in mathematics and science is on concepts and theories rather than their diverse realizations, excellence has to be designed into the teaching materials. How to achieve such excellence is less well understood, or researched – partly because its importance is not widely recognized in education.

Design skill can be developed but it is partly innate, born not made. It grows with experience over many years. Outstanding designers seem to work in different ways, some being mainly driven by theoretical ideas, others by previous exemplars, or by inspiration from the world around them. All have the ability to integrate multiple inputs to their imagination. All have deep understanding of the craft skills of the environment they design for – mathematics or science teaching, for example. Quality seems to lie in combining specific learning foci with a rich complexity of connections to other ideas, integrated in a natural-seeming way that feels easy in use. Not so different from literature and music.

Design excellence is recognizable; people tend to agree on which products show design flair. At the present crude level of understanding of design, the best advice to project leaders and institutions is heuristic – look for outstanding designers, and give them an environment in which they flourish and develop. Above all, if you want outstanding products, don't overdirect designers with detailed design objectives and constraints; balancing and fine-tuning can be done later by other, analytic minds. Keep each design team small so that communication is through day-by-day conversation, rather than management structures. (The extraordinary research creativity of Xerox PARC was achieved with a maximum of ten people per research team.)

The stages of the design phase are typically:

- outlining an agreement with the client on the broad goals and structure of the product;

- generating design ideas within the design group, in consultation with experts and outstanding practitioners; and
- drafting materials, which are tried out in the target arena (for example, classrooms) by the lead designer and others in the design group, then revised, producing the all-important 'alpha version'.

In practice, as always with creative processes, there is cycling among these stages.

Design control is a concept we at the Shell Centre have found to be important to the progress of any project. The principle is that one person, after appropriate consultation with the team, takes all the design decisions on the aspect they control. This has two major advantages. It retains design coherence, which improves quality, and it avoids extended debates in the search for consensus, which saves time and energy. If a consensus is clear in discussion, the designer is expected to follow it – or have a very good explanation for doing something else. (Everyone is expected to take very seriously the empirical feedback from the trials.)

NTPS moved through the design phase in the following way. In the mid-1980s, there was general discontent with the national system of assessment in mathematics at age sixteen, stimulated by the Cockcroft Report (1979). There was an opportunity to try new examinations, linked to a recognition that the academic remoteness of mathematics was not ideal or essential – that functional mathematics should be tried. I proposed to the Joint Matriculation Board that the Shell Centre team should develop a new assessment with them and, because it breaks new ground, teaching materials to enable teachers to prepare for it. We agreed on five to ten 3-week modules, each with its own assessment, both during the module and afterwards.

We assembled a group of six innovative teachers and, with a few outside experts on mathematics education, held a series of brainstorming sessions on topics from the outside world that might make good modules. About thirty topics were considered; individuals or pairs drafted rough few-page outlines for each topic. After much discussion, we settled on ten topics for further exploratory development, with a fairly clear view of their order. (In the end, there were five.)

Design control was clarified. Malcolm Swan would lead the design, particularly of the student materials and assessment tasks. John Gillespie organized the trials and relations with schools, and led the design of one module. Barbara Binns wrote notes for teachers, and managed the development process, including links with the examination board. I led on strategic issues (for example, an initial challenge was to ensure that the design remained focused on the *unfamiliar* goal, functional mathematics in the service of real problem solving, rather than reverting to 'just mathematics'), on the overall structure of the product, and how we would get there. Everyone contributed ideas and suggestions on all aspects of the work.

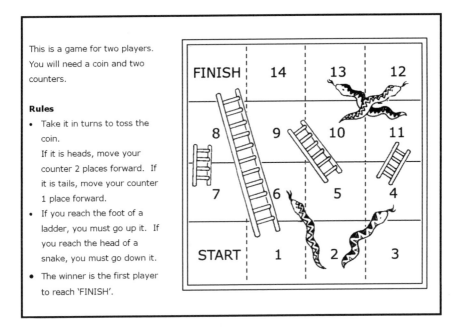

This is a game for two players. You will need a coin and two counters.

Rules

- Take it in turns to toss the coin.
  If it is heads, move your counter 2 places forward. If it is tails, move your counter 1 place forward.
- If you reach the foot of a ladder, you must go up it. If you reach the head of a snake, you must go down it.
- The winner is the first player to reach 'FINISH'.

Figure 9.2 Snakes and Ladders assessment task

In understanding the challenge of this kind of problem, we decided to break each module into four stages, characteristic of good problem solving: understanding the problem situation; brainstorming; detailed design and planning; implementation and evaluation. A key challenge in all investigative work is to sustain students' autonomy as problem solvers, without their losing their way or being discouraged. We decided that students should work in groups of three or four, guided by a student booklet. Individual assessment at the end of each stage would monitor the understanding of each student. Among many design details, the booklet gave strategic guidance on what to do in each stage, with delayed checklists to ensure that nothing essential had been overlooked.

'Design a board game' was chosen as the first module to develop. Understanding of what this involves was achieved by creating a series of amusingly bad board games for the students to play, critique, and improve. (The students were delighted that these 'wrong answers' came from the examination board – an unexpected bonus.) The *Snakes and Ladders* assessment task in Figure 9.2 exemplifies this.

They now understood that a game needs a board and a set of rules, it should be fair – and should end in a reasonable time! Each group then enjoyed exploring a range of ideas. The design and construction of their board, and testing the game followed. (In one enterprising trial school, this became a joint project with the art department.) Evaluation was accomplished by each group playing the other groups' games, commenting on them, and voting for a favourite. Notes for teachers had been built up by the team through this tryout process. These and the student books were revised and assembled into first draft form, ready for trials.

The 'final examinations' were designed rather later. There were two papers for each module, called Standard and Extension Levels, which assessed the student's ability to transfer what they had learnt, to less- and more-remote problem situations respectively. These were externally scored by the board. Basic level was awarded on the basis of the assessment tasks embedded in the teaching materials. Assessing the group's products was seen as a step too far.

To summarize, it is the integration of research-based design principles and excellence in design with appropriate educational goals that produces really exceptional educational products.

Systematic iterative development

The design process produces draft materials. The team has some evidence on the response of students, albeit with atypical teachers (the authors), but none on how well the materials transfer, helping other teachers create comparable learning experiences in their classrooms. It is systematic development that turns drafts into robust and effective products. It involves successive rounds of trials, with rich and detailed feedback, in increasingly realistic circumstances.

The feedback at each stage guides the revision of the materials by the design team. Feedback can take many forms; the criterion for choosing what information to collect is its usefulness for that purpose. This also depends on presenting it in a form that the designers can readily absorb – too much indigestible information is as useless as too little; equally, it depends on the designers' willingness to learn from feedback, and having the skills to infer appropriate design changes from it. Cost-effectiveness then implies different balances of feedback at each stage. In the development of teaching materials, these typically include alpha trials, followed by discussion, and then beta trials, followed by discussion, until the final version is ready for publication.

Alpha trials were held in a handful of classrooms (normally five to ten), some with robust teachers who can handle anything and others more typical of the target group. This small number is enough to allow observers to distinguish those things that are generic, found in most of the classrooms, from those that are idiosyncratic. The priority at this stage is the quality of feedback from each classroom, including:

- structured observation reports by a team of observers, covering in detail every lesson of each teacher;
- samples of student work, for analysis by the team; and

- informal-but-structured interviews with teachers and students on their overall response to the lesson, and on the details of the lesson materials, line by line.

The process of communicating what has been found to the designers is important, and difficult to optimize. We like to have meetings, in which the observers share their information with the lead designer in two stages presenting: first, an analytic picture of each teacher in the trials, working without and with the new materials; then, a line-by-line discussion of the materials, bringing out what happened in each of the classrooms, noting where the materials did not communicate effectively to teacher or students and how the intended activities worked out. The discussion in these sessions is primarily about clarifying the meaning of the data, but suggestions for revision also flow. The role of the lead designer in this process is that of listener and questioner, absorbing the information and suggestions, and integrating them into decisions on revision.

Revision by the lead designer follows this discussion, producing the 'beta version'. The priorities are different now, focused on the realization of the lessons in typical classrooms. A larger sample (twenty to fifty) is needed. It should be roughly representative of the target groups. (We have usually obtained stratified, reasonably random samples by invitation – "You have been chosen ...." has good acceptance rates, particularly when the materials can be related to high-stakes assessment.) Within given team resources, a larger sample means more limited feedback from each classroom, largely confined to written material from samples of students. Observation of the beta version in use in another small group of classrooms is an important complement to this.

Revision by the lead designer again follows, producing the final version for publication. The development of NTPS worked very much in this way. Numerous improvements were made as the result of the feedback from the alpha trials, some removing 'bugs' in the activities themselves, or in the teacher's misunderstanding of the guidance, others incorporating good ideas that emerged from individual classrooms. The beta trials were mostly checking and validating what we had learnt with the larger sample – they produced many small changes. The evaluative feedback we received provided a substantial basis for a summative view of the outcomes, positive in terms of student achievement and (vividly) of attitude to mathematics. A notable feature was the narrowing gap between previously high- and low-performing students – an important equity goal that is notoriously hard to achieve. It seemed to arise largely from discomfort with non-routine tasks for some, and improved motivation for others. Because of pressures and priorities, none of this data was collected in a sufficiently structured way for a research journal – a defect, common in such work, that one would like to have the time and resources to overcome.

This is not the end of the process. Feedback 'from the field' will guide future developments. Both informal comments from users and more structured research will produce insights on which to build. Changing circumstances may lead to further development of the product. NTPS, with its own examination, was sidelined by the introduction of the GCSE as a universal examination at age sixteen. To continue to serve the schools that had become enthusiastic about this functional approach to mathematics, we and the examination board developed a GCSE built around it. As so often, fitting into this new framework led to compromises and some distortion of the approach, with more emphasis on imitative exercises rather than mathematics in use.

Such an engineering research methodology is common in many fields for the development of tools and processes so as to ensure that they work well for their intended users and purposes. It is still often neglected in education for the craft-based approach, which may be summarized as: write draft materials from your own experience; circulate to an expert group; discuss at meetings; revise; publish. This is quicker and cheaper, but does not allow substantial innovations that work effectively for the whole target community of users.

Weak design and development can produce costly flaws. (For example, the unintended consequences of pressure for 'simple tests' in mathematics include a destructive fragmentation of learning as teachers 'teach to the test'.) And it is well known in engineering that the later a flaw is detected, the more it costs to fix – more by orders of magnitude!

Comparative in-depth evaluation

This third key element in the engineering approach is also the least developed.[6] It is nonetheless critically important for *policy makers and practitioners*, guiding choices of materials and approaches, and for *design teams*, informing product improvement and future developments. For the first of these, evaluation needs to be seen to be independent; for both it needs to look in depth at: (1) widely available treatments, competing in the same area; (2) all important variables: types of user, styles of use, and levels of support (professional development etc.); (3) outcome measures that cover the full range of design intentions, including classroom activities as well as student performance; and (4) alternative products, their approaches and detailed engineering.

The scale implied in this specification explains why, as far as I know, there has been no such study, anywhere in the world, although the research skills it needs are in the mainstream of current educational research.

In a back-of-the-envelope look at what such a study in the United States of America might entail, I estimate:

- Time scale: year 1 preparation and recruiting; year 2 piloting, schools start curriculum; year 3–6 data capture; year 4–7 analysis and publication; year 5–7 curriculum revision; then loop to year 3 with some new materials;

- Grade range: three middle grades, ages 11–14 (others a year or two behind);
- Curricula: nine diverse published curricula; two or three focal units per year in each curriculum;
- School systems: ten nationwide, diverse, subject to agreement to go with the methodology;
- Schools and classrooms: two classrooms per grade in ten schools per system, assigned in pairs to five of the curricula "by invitation," with levels of professional development and other support that the school system agrees to reproduce on large-scale implementation; and
- Data: Pre-, post- and delayed-test scores on a broad range of assessment instruments; ongoing samples of student work; classroom observation of ten lessons per year in each class, with post-interviews; pre-, post- and delayed-questionnaires on beliefs, style and attitudes.

A rough estimate of the cost of such an exercise focuses on lesson observation, the most expensive component. Assuming one observer–researcher for eight classrooms (that is, eighty observations per year, plus all the other work), this implies for each grade range: 10 school systems × 20 classrooms × 3 grades/8 = 75 researchers @ $100K per year ~$10 million a year for the 3 main years (three to six) of the study ~$30 million including leadership, support and overhead. With five universities involved, each would need a team of about fifteen people covering the necessary range of research, development and system skills. This is, indeed, 'big education' – but likely to be cost-effective (see later section on the costs of good engineering, p. 146).

Functional mathematics will need this kind of evaluation in due time, bearing in mind that a typical time from agreeing goals to stable curriculum implementation is approximately ten years. Meanwhile, it represents a research and development challenge.

Systematic development of models for system change

In the introduction, I noted the need for reliable, research-based models of the overall process of educational change – approaches that are validated, not merely by *post hoc* analyses but by evidential warrants for robustness that policy makers can rely on. This is clearly a challenging design and development problem. Nowhere has it been solved for the kind of educational changes that research has shown to be essential for high-quality learning, at least in mathematics and science. Some progress has been made, giving reasonable hope that a similar developmental approach can succeed.

Here the system of study is much more complex (even) than the classroom or the professional development of teachers, involving a much broader range of key players – students, teachers, principals, professional leadership, system administrators, politicians and the public. As with any planned change, all of the key groups must move in the way intended, if the outcomes are to resemble the intentions.

There are now well-engineered exemplars of many of the key elements in such a change. Some are familiar tools – classroom teaching materials, and assessment that will encourage and reward aspects of performance that reflect the new goals, have long been recognized as essential support for large-scale change. In recent years, tools have been developed in some other areas that have previously been seen as inevitably craft-based. For example, materials to support specific kinds of 'live' professional development have been developed, and shown to enable less-experienced leaders to replace experts without substantial 'loss' to the participants. Given that there are a thousand mathematics teachers for every such expert, this is an important step forward in seeking large-scale improvement.

The focus has now moved beyond such specific areas to the change process itself. Until now, support for systems has been in the form of general advice and occasional 'technical assistance' by 'experts'. We have begun to develop a 'Toolkit for Change Agents' (see www.toolkitforchange .org), which aims to suggest successful *strategies* for responding to the common *challenges* that inevitably arise in every improvement program, and the *tools* that each employs. The entries in the toolkit are based on the successful experience of other 'change agents' who faced similar challenges. This work is still at an early stage but shows promise of helping with this core problem.

However, my purpose here is mainly to draw attention to the educational change process as an area that needs more than the critical commentary that has guided it so far. Because the system of study is larger than a student or a classroom, with more obviously important variables, the challenge to systematic research and development is greater. However, it is surely possible to provide those seeking to promote improvement with well-engineered tools that will increase their effectiveness, founded on research-based insights into the processes of change. This, too, will need large-scale projects.

Building the skill base for engineering research

The number of groups capable of high-quality engineering is now small and, as we have noted, they are far from secure. If the research-based approach is to become a substantial and effective part of large-scale improvement, the number of those who can do such work will need to grow. This will involve both finding and training people with specific skills and creating institutional structures that can handle such work as well as the teams of people with complementary skills that it requires. This takes time, typically a decade or so, fortunately matching the time any new approach will need to build public confidence in its value. We also need to bear in mind the changing balance of work.

Four levels of R&D – improving balance

I noted that a focus on improving practice will need a different balance of effort among the research styles presented earlier (insight versus impact), with more engineering research. A complementary perspective on balance is provided by looking at different 'levels' of research (R) and development (D), summarized in Table 9.1.

Note the crucial difference between ET, which is about teaching possibilities, usually explored by a member of the research team, and RT, which is about what can be achieved in practice by typical teachers with realistic levels of support. Note how the research foci, R in the third column, change across the levels. Currently, nearly all research is at L and ET levels. A better balance across the levels is needed, if research and practice are to benefit from each other as they could. The main contribution of design research has been to link the R and D elements in the third column – but, in most cases, only for the first two levels, L and ET. Both RT and SC research need larger

Table 9.1 Four levels of R&D

Level	Variables	Typical research and development foci
Learning (L)	Student	R: concepts, skills strategies, metacognition
	Task	D: learning situations, probes, data capture
Exceptional Teacher (ET)	Instruction	R: teaching tactics + strategies, nature of student learning
	Student	
	Task	D: classroom materials for some teachers
Representative Teacher (RT)	Teacher	R: performance of representative teachers with realistic support; basic studies of teacher competencies
	Instruction	
	Student	D: classroom materials that 'work' for most teachers
	Task	
System Change (SC)	System	R: system change
	School	D: 'Tools for Change', i.e. materials for: classrooms, assessment, professional development, community relations
	Teacher	
	Instruction	
	Student	
	Task	

research teams and longer time scales, which is difficult to accommodate within typical academic structures, current in education.

What skills, and where will they come from?

In the first section (p. 122) I noted the key groups of contributors. Let us look at where they are needed, and where they will come from.

Insight-focused researchers with the necessary range of skills for their roles in the engineering approach already exist in large numbers in universities; the challenge, to create an academic climate that will encourage them to do such work, is discussed in the next section.

Designer–developers of high quality are rare,[9] partly because of the lack of any career path, from apprentice to expert professional, that encourages this activity; the development of this area, and the understanding of design skill in education, is still at an early stage. Progress in this area will be an important factor in the whole enterprise (Gardner and Shulman 2005). An International Society for Design and Development in Education (ISDDE; www .ISDDE.org) has recently been founded with the goals of:

- improving the design and development process
- building a design and development community
- increasing the impact of this on educational practice.

Project leaders are a similarly rare species, for much the same reasons – the multidimensional skills needed for this work are fairly well understood but, even with a supportive environment, it will take time to develop project leaders within the design and development community with experience in educational engineering.

Client funders with understanding of good engineering will appear as its potential is recognized – indeed, the scale of the funding of long-term coherent programs may be the best measure of progress; the ability of the engineering community to demonstrate this potential through funded projects will be crucial to justifying expansion.

All of these groups play vital roles. In the following section, we look at the changes that are needed in their current working environments to make progress possible.

Changing behaviour in academia, industry and governments

If these things were happening in major education systems, there would be no need for this paper. My colleagues and I could just concentrate on good engineering. Currently, moving from the present to the kind of approach outlined above will require change by all the key players in educational innovation. It is simplest to discuss them in reverse order.

Governments

Experience in other fields suggests that substantial government funding will flow into research in education, if and when policy makers and the public become convinced that the research community can deliver clear and important practical benefits to the system. (*IER* discusses this in some detail.) Medical research only received significant support from the early twentieth century on, as research-based benefits such as X-rays began to appear. Massive support followed the impact of penicillin and other antibiotics after 1945, perhaps helped by the drama of its discovery by Alexander Fleming. Physics too, particularly nuclear physics, was a fairly abstruse field until that time. (The annual budget in the 1930s of the world-leading Cavendish Laboratory under Rutherford was about £3,000 – peanuts by today's standards, even in real terms.) The role of physicists in World War II in the development of radar, operations research, nuclear weapons and many other things increased funding for pure, as well as applied, physics research by many orders of magnitude – a situation that continues to this day. (It has also continued to spin off practical benefits, including the founders of molecular biology, the Internet, and the World Wide Web.)

However, in most of these cases, government played a crucial pump-priming role, providing funding for 'proof of concept' studies while the practical benefits were still unproven. That will be necessary in education; however, it will only make sense to policy makers if credible structures are in place that give real promise of clear and direct practical benefits in the medium term. This will need a growing body of exemplar products of well-recognized effectiveness.

Industry

Here there is a different problem. In medicine and engineering, for example, there are industries that turn the prototypes of academic research into fully developed practical tools and processes. Pharmaceuticals and electronics are two obvious examples but the same is true across manufacturing industry. Firms have established links with academic researchers in their fields; they support pure research and the research-based development of prototypes. The firms then take these through the long and costly process of development into robust products.

No comparable industry exists in education. The publishing industry (the obvious candidate) turns prototypes (manuscripts) into products (books), but with minimal development – typically comments by a few 'experts' and a small-scale trial with teachers who, again, are simply asked to comment. Neither you nor the regulator would allow your children to be treated with a drug, or fly in a plane, that had been developed like this. It produces products that *work*, in some sense, but it is no way to break new ground with products that are really effective – both well designed and robust in use.[10]

Why is this so? The main reason is the continuing dominance of the craft-based approach, surviving largely because of the inadequate evaluation process. There is no systematic independent testing and reporting on the effectiveness of products. New teaching materials *are* regularly reviewed – but by an 'expert' who must deliver the review in a week or two, purely on the basis of inspection. The improved effectiveness produced by development often depends on quite subtle refinements; it only shows when representative samples of users (for example, typical teachers and students, working with the materials), are studied in depth. As we have noted, such studies take time and cost money. The situation is exacerbated because the *buyer* and the *user* of many products are different – for example, the school system buys the teaching materials that the teachers use. Marketing is, of course, aimed at the buyer. Given this situation, there is a greater need, and responsibility, for the academic community to do this kind of work – and for governments to fund it.[11] It goes almost without saying that there are no regulatory agencies on the lines of those that every country has for drugs and for aeroplanes.

Thus, currently there is no incentive for industry to invest in systematic development. Systematic evaluation, preferably before marketing, would change that; it would increase the cost of materials but not to a strategically significant extent (see the next section, p. 146).

Academia

If the situation is to improve, major changes will need to come in academia. Currently the *academic value system in education*, which controls academic appointments and promotions, is actively hostile to engineering research. As discussed in *IER*, it favours:

- new ideas *over* reliable research
- new results *over* replication and extension
- trustworthiness *over* generalizability
- small studies *over* major programs
- personal research *over* team research
- first author *over* team member
- disputation *over* consensus building
- journal papers *over* products and processes.

Schoenfeld (2002) describes most such studies as of 'limited generality but … (if properly done) … "here is something worth paying attention to"'. As I have noted, that is a totally inadequate basis for design. In all respects these values undermine research that would have clear impact on the improvement of teaching and learning.

A status pattern, where the pure is valued far more than the applied, is common but it is not general at any level of research. Many Nobel Prizes are for the design and development of devices – for example, only two people have won *two* Nobel Prizes in the same field: John Bardeen, the physicist, for the *transistor*, and for the *theory of superconductivity* and Fred Sanger, the biologist, for the *3D structure of haemoglobin* (a first in this application of X-ray crystallography) and for *the procedure for sequencing DNA*.

At least two of these are engineering in approach. With examples like these, education need not fear for its respectability in giving equal status to engineering research. These lie in 'Pasteur's Quadrant' (Stokes 1997) of work that contributes both practical benefits and new insights. However, one should not undervalue work in Edison's Quadrant, with its purely practical focus – contributions like the luminous filament light bulb are of inestimable social value. Note also that, in making this discovery, Edison investigated and catalogued the properties of hundreds of other candidate materials, adding to the body of phenomenological knowledge that is part of the theoretical underpinning of all engineering. In contrast, so much research in education lies in the quadrant that has no name – advancing neither theory nor practice.

Changing the culture in any established profession is notoriously difficult. What actions may help to bring this about in educational research? Leaders in the academic research community can make a major contribution by including direct impact on practice as a key criterion for judging research, complementing valid current criteria. One may (hopefully) envisage a future search committee at an academic institution that wants to hire a senior person in education, and is mindful of public pressure to *make a difference*. The institution has decided that candidates must either be outstanding on one of the following criteria, or be very strong on two or three:

- Impact on practice: evidence should cover the number of teachers and students directly affected; the nature of the improvement sought and achieved; specific expressions of interest in future development;
- Contribution to theory and/or knowledge: evidence should cover how new or synthetic the work is; warrants for trustworthiness, generality, and importance; citations; reviews; how frequently researchers elsewhere have used the ideas; and
- Improvement in either research or design methodology: evidence should cover how far the new approaches are an improvement on previous approaches; in what ways the work is robust, and applies to new situations; to what degree others employ these methods.

Given the self-interest of those who are successful under current criteria, progress in this area will not be easy; however, real leaders often have the necessary confidence to promote principled improvements. Funding agencies can play their part, as they currently do, by funding projects that require good engineering. Furthermore, they can encourage universities to give successful teams, *including their designers*, long-term appointments.

What does good engineering cost?

It is clear that the process of design and development outlined earlier (systematic design, development and evaluation) is more expensive than the simple author → publisher chain of the craft-based approach. How much does it cost? How does this investment in R&D compare with that in other fields where improvement is needed?

The NSF-funded projects for developing mathematics curriculum materials in the 1990s were each funded at a level of about $1,000,000 for each year's materials, supporting about 200 hours of teaching – that is, about $5,000 per classroom hour. Each team worked under enormous pressure to deliver at the required rate of one year's material per project year. At the Shell Centre, we have tackled less-forbidding challenges. We have developed smaller units, each supporting about 15 hours, at typical cost of £7,000–15,000 ($15,000–30,000) per classroom hour. The difference, and the range, reflects the amount of feedback, particularly classroom observation, that the funding and time has enabled. The cost of the full process (as outlined in the design, development and evaluation section, p. 132) is at the top of this range.

What would the redevelopment of the whole school curriculum cost at $30,000 per classroom hour? (No one is suggesting that everything needs to change but this gives an upper limit to the total cost.) Let us assume

- 14 years of schooling × 200 days per year × 5 hours per day = 14,000 hours
- 3 parallel developments to meet different student needs > 40,000 hours
- $30,000 per classroom hour for high-quality development

which gives a total of approximately $1.2 billion. Spread over, say, 5 years – the minimum time such a development effort would need – that yields an R&D cost of $120 million per year; since the annual expenditure on schools in the United States of America is at least $300 billion, this amounts to *investing ~0.04% of total running cost in R&D*.

Any measurable gain in the effectiveness or efficiency of schooling would justify this expenditure. (It could be saved by increasing the average number of students in a school of 2,500 students by just one student!)

For smaller countries, the proportion would be higher but still modest.

For comparison, other fields that are developing rapidly typically spend 5 per cent to 15 per cent of turnover on R&D, with 80 per cent on research-based development, 20 per cent on basic research. I believe that a level of 1 per cent of such investment in education is an appropriate target for many advanced countries. This would cover not only the R&D but the (larger) extra-implementation costs, involving as it must networks of 'live' support. This would transform the quality of children's education, with consequent benefits in personal satisfaction and economic progress.

All this takes time. However, government are used to planning and funding long-term projects in other fields – 4 years to plan and 5 years to build a bridge or an aeroplane.

Implications for policy and the design community

In this chapter, we have seen how an engineering research approach may enable

research insights ⇒ better tools and processes ⇒ improved practice

through creative design and systematic refinement using research methods. Achieving this will need changes at policy level in the strategies for educational improvement; each of these changes will depend on active effort by the research and development communities. To summarize, the strategic changes that seem to be needed are:

- Recognition that good engineering is valuable and weak engineering costly. Good engineering produces more effective and reliable outcomes, which justify the higher cost and longer time scales than the craft-based approach; persuasive evidence on this can only come from independent comparative in-depth evaluation of widely available products in use in realistic circumstances – a smarter buyer will then support better design. This needs a substantial effort by research communities, and appropriate funding.
- Coherent planning and funding of improvement by school systems, combining the long time scales of substantial educational improvement with demonstrable year-by-year gains that will satisfy political needs; the design and development community can help by linking its responses to short-term funding opportunities to a realistic long-term vision, negotiated with funders and based on basic research and past successes.
- Substantial multiskilled teams of designers, developers, evaluators and other insight researchers capable of carrying through such major projects with the long time scales they imply; while specialist centres

will continue to play an important role, there is a need for universities to play the central role they do in other 'big' fields such as physics and medicine (recognition, see above, will be important in persuading governments to make the investment needed).

- Broadening of the academic value system in universities, giving equal research credit to in-depth insights and impact on practice; this will need leadership from the research community and pressure from funders.
- Building credible theories of learning and teaching to guide research-based design and development that links to that of insight-focused research and, in turn, drives the latter to build a consensus-based core of results that are well-specified and reliable enough to be a useful basis for design.
- Collaboration: all the above will be advanced if funders, project leaders, designers and researchers learn to work more closely together over time; while the community of researchers is long established, the design and development community in education has still to acquire similar coherence.

Clearly, there is much that is challenging to be accomplished here. But, if governments and other funders become convinced that we can deliver what they need then, together, we can make educational research a more useful, more influential, and much better-funded enterprise.

Acknowledgements

The analysis in this paper owes much to discussions with Phil Daro, Alan Schoenfeld, Kaye Stacey and my colleagues at the Shell Centre – Alan Bell, Malcolm Swan, and Daniel Pead.

Notes

1 Some of the work reported in earlier chapters *is* 'engineering research' – but most of it is not. The term 'design research' covers a very wide range and I hope to show that the distinction is important.
2 The Shell Centre, also founded about 40 years ago with similar goals, has a team of about 5 people and lives from project to project on short-term funds. Sustaining long-term strategies for improvement in these circumstances requires stubborn selectivity – and luck.
3 UK university departments in all subjects undergo a Research Assessment Exercise (RAE) every 6 years. This was the definition of research for the RAE.
4 There are some areas where the need for careful *development* is recognized, notably in the development of tests; here the results have not been encouraging, largely because the *design* has often been approached on a narrow basis, dominated by traditional psychometrics, with little attention to whether what is

actually assessed truly reflects the learning goals of the subject in a balanced way. Cognitive science research and better design are both needed here.

5 The difference between Mozart and Salieri, and the hundreds of little-known composers from that time, was not in their theoretical principles; it was what each did with them. The principles and rules of melody, harmony and counterpoint were well known to, and used by, all of them.

6 The US 'What Works Clearinghouse' in its study of mathematics teaching materials, the most active area of materials development, found no study of this kind to review – this in a country with tens of thousands of educational researchers, many of them evaluators (see Schoenfeld 2006).

7 The issues of sampling, random or matched assignment need ongoing study and experiment.

8 These can also be designed to probe teachers' 'pedagogical content knowledge' of mathematics or science.

9 After many years of searching for outstanding designers, I know of only a few tens in mathematics education worldwide with whom I would be keen to work.

10 It is true that some educational software is developed somewhat more systematically – the inevitably high cost of design and programming makes room for this. However, even this is held back by the same lack of reliable data for users on how well it works.

11 The 'What Works Clearinghouse' in the US has such a purpose; the methodology is profoundly flawed (see Schoenfeld (2006)) – but perhaps it is a start.

References

Bell, A. (1993). Some experiments in diagnostic teaching. *Educational Studies in Mathematics*, 24(1), 115–37. Also URL: www.toolkitforchange.org

Burkhardt, H. and Schoenfeld, A. H. (2003). Improving educational research: Towards a more useful, more influential and better funded enterprise. *Educational Researcher*, 32(9), 3–14.

Cockcroft Report (1979). *Mathematics Counts*. London: HMSO.

Gardner, H. and Shulman, L. S. (2005). *The Professions in America Today* (and other articles on *Professions and Professionals*). Daedalus, Summer 2005.

HEFC (1999). *Guidance on Submissions to the Research Assessment Exercise* (paragraph 1.12). London: Higher Education Funding Council for England and Wales 1999. URL: www.hero.ac.uk/rae/

OECD (2003). *The PISA 2003 assessment framework: Mathematics, reading science and problem solving knowledge and skills*, Paris. URL: https://www.pisa.oecd.org/dataoecd/38/51/33707192.pdf

RAE (Research Assessment Exercise) (2001). Research assessment exercise 2001: Briefing notes. URL: http://195.194.167.103/Pubs/2_01

Schoenfeld, A. H. (2002). Research methods in (mathematics) education. In L. English (ed.), *Handbook of International Research in Mathematics Education* (pp. 435–88). Mahwah, NJ: Erlbaum.

Schoenfeld, A. H. (2006). What doesn't work: The challenge and failure of the what works clearinghouse to conduct meaningful reviews of studies of mathematics curricula. *Educational Researcher* 35(2), 13–21.

Shell Centre (1987–89), Swan, M., Binns, B., Gillespie, J., and Burkhardt, H., *Numeracy Through Problem Solving* (five modules for curriculum and assessment in mathematical literacy). Harlow: Longman, revised Shell Centre Publications, Nottingham, UK, 2000. URL: www.mathshell.com/scp/index.htm

Stokes, D. E. (1997). *Pasteur's Quadrant: Basic Science and Technical Innovation.* Washington, DC: Brookings.

Tomlinson Report (2004). *14–19 Curriculum and Qualifications Reform.* Department for Education and Skills. London: HMSO. URL: www.14–19reform.gov.uk

Chapter 10

Educational design research

The value of variety

*Nienke Nieveen, Susan McKenney and
Jan van den Akker*

This book has offered a platform for discussing educational design research, and several views on how to assess and assure its quality. In this closing chapter, we explore the role that design research plays in the broader scientific cycle, including implications for assessing the quality of design research proposals, activities, and reports.

The scientific cycle

The discussion in this chapter departs from the contribution made by Phillips in Chapter 6, where he expresses concern about "serious oversimplification" of scientifically oriented research. He points to the contemporary trend to primarily emphasize the final stage of the research cycle – testing claims of causality (for example, randomized field trials). He also reminds readers about the importance of the preliminary investigation stage that is guided by deep factual and theoretical understanding. In so doing, he indicates that a view of science as proceeding through several stages has been well established for quite some time, citing writings of Reichenbach, Popper, and Dewey as examples. With regard to educational design research, Kelly (Chapter 8) and Bannan-Ritland (2003) point to the need to see design research as an integral approach within a larger scientific cycle.

Figure 10.1 is based on the notion that scientific inquiry in general, and educational research in particular, flows through multiple cycles. It shows that earlier stages share an *exploratory emphasis* including speculation, observation, identification of variables/processes, modeling, prototyping, and initial implementation. Design research is conducted within or across these stages. Later stages share a *confirmatory emphasis*, in which causality is tested. This may range from smaller-scale learning experiments through large-scale diffusion and comparative testing of impact. Here, effect studies, such as randomized field trials, are conducted. The exploratory emphasis is necessary to arrive at well-designed innovations, worthy of going to scale, and the confirmatory emphasis is necessary not only to test the impact of an innovation, but also to provide sound inputs for future exploratory work.

Design research differentiation

The contributions within this book discuss varying perspectives on design research. While all the chapters touch on the exploratory nature of design research, variations do exist. In exploring that variation, particularly when revisiting the variation in design aims, we find it useful to distinguish between studies that aim to (dis)prove learning theories – *validation studies* and those that aim to solve an educational problem using relevant theoretical knowledge – *development studies*. Whereas both types involve the design, development, and evaluation of learning innovations in context, their scientific output differs. As elaborated under the next heading, validation studies ultimately contribute most to advancing (domain-specific) instructional theories, while development studies yield design principles for use in solving education problems.

Validation studies

Validation studies feature the design of learning trajectories in order to develop, elaborate, and validate theories about both the process of learning and the resulting implications for the design of learning environments. In this category, we draw parallels with well-known works such as those of Brown (1992) and Collins (1992), as well as newer ones from this volume (Chapters 2 and 3). With the aim of advancing learning theory, validation studies contribute to several levels of theory development (Chapter 3):

- microtheories: at the level of the instructional activities;
- local instruction theories: at the level of the instructional sequence; and
- domain-specific instruction theory: at the level of pedagogical content knowledge.

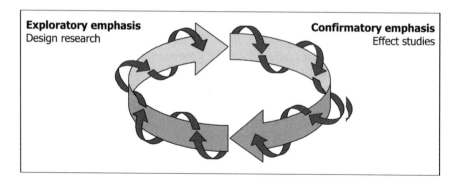

Figure 10.1 Design research within the scientific cycle

In order to reach these aspirations, researchers deliberately choose naturally occurring test beds (though they tend to work with above-average teaching staff) instead of laboratory or simulated settings. In doing so, their work evolves through several stages (Chapter 3) such as:

- Environment preparation: elaborating a preliminary instructional design based on an interpretative framework;
- Classroom experiment: testing and improving the instructional design/local instructional theory and developing an understanding of how it works; and
- Retrospective analysis: studying the entire data set to contribute to the development of a local instructional theory and (improvement of) the interpretative framework.

DiSessa and Cobb (2004: 83) warn that "design research will not be particularly progressive in the long run if the motivation for conducting experiments is restricted to that of producing domain specific instructional theories." A practical contribution of validation studies lies in the development and implementation of specific learning trajectories that were implemented to test the theoretical basis of the design.

Development studies

Whereas the practical contribution is a (secondary) benefit of most validation studies, derivation of design principles for use in practice is a fundamental aim of most development studies. Here, research is problem-driven, situated in the educational field, and involves close interaction between practitioners, researchers, experts, and other stakeholders. Design studies of this nature have been described previously (McKenney and van den Akker 2005; Nieveen and van den Akker 1999; Richey and Nelson 1996; Richey *et al.* 2004; van den Akker 1999) as well as in this volume (Chapters 4, 5, and 7)). Development studies integrate state-of-the-art knowledge from prior research in the design process and fine-tune educational innovations based on piloting in the field. Throughout the process, implicit and explicit design decisions are captured. By unpacking the design process, design principles that can inform future development and implementation decisions are derived. Two main types of principles are addressed (Chapters 5 and 7; van den Akker 1999): (1) procedural design principles: characteristics of the design approach; and (2) substantive design principles: characteristics of the design itself.

Since design principles are not intended as recipes for success, but as heuristic guidelines to help others select and apply the most appropriate knowledge for a specific design task in another setting, comprehensive and accurate portrayal of the context is an essential companion to both types of design principles. It should be noted that development studies do more than *merely* demonstrate local utility. As Barab and Squire (2004: 8) put it, "design scientists must draw connections to theoretical assertions and claims that transcend the local context."

In order to solve educational problems and arrive at design principles, development studies usually progress through several stages, as described in Chapters 2, 5, and 7:

- Preliminary research: thorough context and problem analysis along with development of a conceptual framework based on literature review;
- Prototyping stage: setting out design guidelines, optimizing prototypes through cycles of design, formative evaluation, and revision;
- Summative evaluation: often explores transferability and scaling, along with (usually small-scale evaluation of) effectiveness; and
- Systematic reflection and documentation: portrays the entire study to support retrospective analysis, followed by specification of design principles and articulation of their links to the conceptual framework.

Development studies rely on local ownership for being able to observe phenomena in their natural settings. This requires a long-term link with practice as time is necessary to fully explore and optimize an intervention, before implementing it in *normal* settings. Collaborative design activities offer outstanding joint professional learning opportunities for researchers and practitioners (Chapter 5).

Why we need variety

We may be able to learn from "sister fields" such as engineering product design and research on diffusion of innovations (Zaritsky *et al.* 2003). As with all design disciplines, *educational engineering* requires varied types of investigations at different stages of an evolving process. Related to this notion, Brown (1992), Burkhardt and Schoenfeld (2003), and Burkhardt (Chapter 9) advocate scaling mechanisms, such as:

- Alpha trials: held under control of the design research team and under ideal circumstances;
- Beta trials: performed at carefully chosen sites with some support; and
- Gamma trials: focusing on widespread adoption with minimal support.

Taking these ideas seriously implies commitment to long-term endeavors that require substantial support from a research program that embraces an

	Design research		Effectiveness research
	Validation studies	*Development studies*	
Design aim	To elaborate and validate theories	To solve educational problems	-
Quality Focus of Design	Theoretical quality of design	Practicality of intervention	Effectiveness of intervention
Knowledge Claim/ Scientific output	Domain-specific instruction theories	Broadly applicable design principles	Evidence of impact of intervention
Methodological Emphasis	Iterative design with small scale testing in research setting (cf. alpha testing with classroom focus)	Iterative development with formative evaluation in various user settings (cf. beta testing in various contexts)	Large scale, comparative field experiments (cf. gamma testing with system-wide focus)
Practical Contribution	Specific learning trajectories for a specific classroom	Implemented interventions in several contexts/classrooms	Evidence-based change at large scale

Figure 10.2 Educational engineering research cycle

overarching vision. Building on earlier work (van den Akker and McKenney 2004), Figure 10.2 illustrates such a vision in which educational engineering departs from a sound theoretical base built by validation studies, develops through practical understanding from development studies, and is tested by effectiveness research. Due to the scope of each study type, most research programs specialize in one area (validation studies, development studies, or effectiveness research).

Understanding and assessing design research quality

While design researchers may find it easy to see their place in a larger framework, such as the one sketched in the previous section, Kelly (2003; Chapter 8) and Phillips (Chapter 6) emphasize that researchers from other well-established traditions are likely to have little tolerance for rival approaches. This poses great challenges for garnering support for a comparatively nascent research approach. The merits of design research can only become evident to *outsiders* when good examples begin to crop up, and these require substantial long-term commitments. Since the majority of gatekeepers to funding and publication opportunities speak alternate "research dialects" (Kelly 2003), the barriers to launching serious, longitudinal design research seem daunting.

How then should we stimulate thoughtful consideration of design research proposals, activities, and manuscripts? For starters, the design research community could become more explicit about the quality standards that it adheres to and wants to be held accountable for (Dede 2004). As mentioned in the first chapter of this book, it was the need for an internal debate on quality assurance that stimulated the Research Council on Educational Research of the Netherlands Foundation for Scientific Research (NWO/

PROO) to invite well-reputed design researchers to participate in a seminar dedicated to the topic. It was the intention of this book to take the dialogue one step further. Now, nearing a close, we draw upon international literature, chapter contributions and discussions from the NWO/PROO seminar to offer some considerations for understanding and assessing design research quality.

Portray design research in perspective

We view the placement of design research at the exploratory side of a larger scientific cycle as crucial to understanding both its worth and merit. The distinction between validation studies and development studies can be useful in furthering more nuanced discussions of design research. Furthermore, demonstrating that exploratory studies provide the necessary inputs for other research approaches (for example, effectiveness research) may begin to facilitate more productive dialogue with those funding agencies and manuscript reviewers who are open to, but not familiar with, design research.

Demonstrate coherent research design

As with other research approaches, the inclusion of a carefully considered, well-informed conceptual or interpretive framework is essential. Due to the scope of design studies, evidence must be provided for how to deal responsibly with large amounts of data (Reeves *et al.* 2005; Richey and Klein 2005) without wasting time, effort, and resources through "massive overkill" (Dede 2004: 107) in terms of data gathering and analysis. Whether through an interpretive framework or other tools, the research design should clarify how data will be analyzed and interpreted. Additionally, research planning should demonstrate intentions of obtaining regular, critical formative feedback. Although less relevant for most validation studies, development study design should evidence a long-term perspective, include scaling options, and address conditions for sustainable implementation.

Support claims for the expected scientific output

The main contributions of the research should be clearly indicated, and warrants must be provided to match each output. Returning to the motives for design research discussed earlier in this book (Chapter 1) three general types of contributions are likely: (i) formulation of education-related theories or principles; (ii) educational improvement with local ownership; (iii) contribution to an understanding of the design process itself.

Exhibit scientific quality of applicants

Design researchers must offer assurance that they are up to the task. A team that includes distributed expertise (for example, strong past performance in the design area and in domain expertise) should be highly regarded. It may even be possible to use portfolios (Chapter 6) for ascertaining design competence. Finally, evidence of a sustainable relationship among an interdisciplinary team (including researchers, practitioners, experts, and other stakeholders) must be provided.

Closing comments

Ideally, participants from the same commissive space should review design research proposals, activities, and publications (Chapter 8). And, according to Edelson (2002), since design research objectives differ from those of a traditional empirical approach, they should not be judged by the same standards. But until the commissive space of design research grows sufficiently and quality standards within the community become widely known and accepted, design researchers must find ways to help other reviewers look beyond their own methodological preferences. Articulation and discussion of standards by which design research ought to be judged are a first step in this direction. Toward that goal, we hope that this book has offered some useful ideas to help advance the field of design research in education.

References

Bannan-Ritland, B. (2003). The role of design in research: The integrative learning design framework. *Educational Researcher*, *32*(1), 21–4.

Barab, S. and Squire, K. (2004). Design-based research: Putting a stake in the ground. *Journal of the Learning Sciences*, *13*(1), 1–14.

Brown, A. L. (1992). Design experiments: Theoretical and methodological challenges in creating complex interventions in classroom settings. *Journal of the Learning Sciences*, *2*(22), 141–78.

Burkhardt, H. and Schoenfeld, A. (2003). Improving educational research: Toward a more useful, more influential and better-funded enterprise. *Educational Researcher*, *32*(9), 3–14.

Collins, A. (1992). Toward a design science of education. In E. Lagemann and L. Shulman (eds), *Issues in Education Research: Problems and Possibilities* (pp. 15–22). San Francisco: Jossey-Bass.

Dede, C. (2004). If design-based research is the answer, what is the question? *Journal of the Learning Sciences*, *13*(1), 105–14.

diSessa, A. A. and Cobb, P. (2004). Ontological innovation and the role of theory in design experiments. *Journal of the Learning Sciences*, *13*(1), 77–103.

Edelson, D. C. (2002). Design research: What we learn when we engage in design. *Journal of the Learning Sciences*, *11*(1), 105–22.

Kelly, A. (2003). Research as design. *Educational Researcher*, *32*(1), 3–4.

McKenney, S. and van den Akker, J. (2005). Computer-based support for curriculum designers: A case of developmental research. *Educational Technology Research and Development*, *53*(2), 41–66.

Nieveen, N. and van den Akker, J. (1999). Exploring the potential of a computer tool for instructional developers. *Educational Technology Research and Development,* 47(3), 77–98.

Reeves, T., Herrington, J., and Oliver, R. (2005). Design research: A socially responsible approach to instructional technology research in higher education. *Journal of Computing in Higher Education,* 16(2), 97–116.

Richey, R. and Klein, J. (2005). Developmental research methods: Creating knowledge from instructional design and development practice. *Journal of Computing in Higher Education,* 16(2), 23–38.

Richey, R., Klein, J. and Nelson, W. (2004). Developmental research: Studies of instructional design and development. In D. Jonassen (ed.), *Handbook of Research for Educational Communications and Technology* (second edition) (pp. 1099–130). Bloomington, IN: Association for Educational Communications & Technology.

Richey, R. and Nelson, W. (1996). Developmental research. In D. Jonassen (ed.), *Handbook of Research for Educational Communications and Technology* (pp. 1213–45). London: Macmillan.

van den Akker, J. (1999). Principles and methods of development research. In J. van den Akker, R. Branch, K. Gustafson, N. Nieveen, and T. Plomp (eds), *Design Approaches and Tools in Education and Training* (pp. 1–15). Dordrecht: Kluwer Academic Publishers.

van den Akker, J. and McKenney, S. (2004). *How can developmental research improve science curriculum policies and practices?* Presentation at the NARST annual meeting, 1–4 April, Vancouver.

Zaritsky, A., Kelly, A., Flowers, W., Rogers, E., and O'Neill, P. (2003). Clinical design sciences: A view from sister design efforts. *Educational Researcher,* 32(1), 32–4.

Index